"*Two Sons and Forty Years* is a compelling read. The business deal-ings in the story and the affected family relationships are common in society, yet rarely addressed in Christian writing and preaching. Moon weaves many plots into his novel, so the environment is rich with intrigue. I found myself wondering how the challenges could successfully resolve, and was relieved to find the ending satisfying."
— *Thayer Willis LCSW*

"I wish I had read this book on my way to the minis-try. What a helpful difference it might have made in my outlook and performance, especially as I related to the busi-ness owners, managers, and financiers in my congregations."
— *Rev. John Killinger, PhD, Author, minister, professor, theologian*

"In *Two Sons*, Robert Moon has revisited two classic sources of tension in human life - the rivalry of brothers and the experience of grace within a family. Moon has created a credible contemporary setting for exploring these themes. His characters, from the harried, over com-mitted pastor with a decent heart to the grieving businessman nurtur-ing old wounds and worries, are recognizably human. It is a clear and engrossing story that will keep you thinking beyond the last page."
— *The Rev. Alex Joyner, United Methodist pastor and author*

"*Two Sons and Forty Years* captures in heartfelt terms that many clergy are both untrained and emotionally unprepared to help the more successful members of their churches. This book should be handed to each clergyperson as part of his or her preparation for ministry."
— *James Grubman, PhD, Family wealth consultant and author*

"This is a captivating novel that will appeal not only to min-isters but lay persons as well as they search for meaning in life."
— *William Powell Tuck, ThD, Seminary professor, former pastor and author*

"The story illumines the disconnect between the idealism within the church and the complexity of the lives of the flock beyond the church doors. The acknowledgment of the in-

herent tension between justice or fairness and grace frames the narrative and challenges us to expand our own vision. "
– **The Rev. Benjamin W. Maas, Rector,** *St. James Episcopal Church, Warrenton, VA*

TWO SONS AND FORTY YEARS

A Novel by

J. ROBERT MOON

HORATIO PUBLISHING

Horatio Publishing
10070 Greenwich Wood
Nokesville, VA 20181
www.horatiopublishing.com

Publisher's Note: This manuscript is a work of fiction. Names, characters, business organizations, places, events, and incidents either are the product of the author's imagination or are used fictitiously. The author's use of names of actual persons (living or dead), places, and characters is not intended to change the fictional character of the work or to disparage any person, company, products or services.

Edited by Ruth Schwartz
Cover Design by Sharon Bieganski-Negron

Ordering Information: Copies can be ordered in bulk directly from the publisher. Special discounts are available on quantity purchases by corporations, associations, and others. For details, contact the "Special Sales Department" at the address above.

Two Sons and Forty Years/J. Robert Moon. -- 1st edition
ISBN: Paperback 978-0-9982673-0-2
ISBN: Hardcover 978-0-9982673-1-9
Library of Congress Control Number: 2016959842

Manufactured in the United States of America

Dedicated
to my wife
the surprise and
delight of my life
MARIANN LYNCH
for the final stretch
of forty years.

CHAPTER ONE

JON

I am deliberately lazy this Monday morning. I need some back porch time before I re-enter the fray.

"It's okay, Jambo," I tell myself. "You've had a demanding week and weekend. What was it? Eighty hours? Take your time, but not the day. Give yourself a breather. How smart of you to look at your calendar last week and block tomorrow off instead of today. No need to waste feeling bad on your day off."

I am not a slacker, mind you. I consider myself a borderline workaholic, so I have earned the right to show up late on Mondays. Okay, I have had my skirmishes with this job. But over the past seven years, I have gained the respect of my congregation. At least, I like to think I have.

My smartphone reads 7:45 a.m. As I sip my second cup of coffee, I recall my first Sunday as the senior pastor at The Summer Hill Memorial Church, affectionately referred to locally as The Hill. Although I stood in the center aisle as Reverend Jonathan A. Boatwright, my palms were sweaty as I lifted the Book of the Gospels over my head. I am so glad I had rehearsed that reading the previous day, testing the microphone system to avoid the damnation of PA feedback. It was the Fourth Sunday in Lent.

"The Holy Gospel of our Lord Jesus, according to Luke," I announced, amazed at the authority of my own voice. I was concerned while reading the ancient passage that some of those in the congregation could even recite it from memory. The words rolled easily from my tongue:

> *"Now all the tax collectors and sinners were coming near to listen to him. And the Pharisees and the scribes were grumbling and saying, 'This fellow welcomes sinners and eats with them.'*
>
> *"So he told them this parable:*
>
> *"There was a man who had two sons. . ."*

When I finished reading the story, I lifted the heavy red and gold book over my head again and proclaimed, "The Gospel of the Lord."

Less than half the audience responded, mumbling, "Praise be to thee, Lord Christ."

I handed the book to my assistant, then with some trepidation, I did something new for this congregation, and for myself. Instead of climbing the four risers to the enclosed pulpit, I stepped to the head of the center aisle and offered the traditional segue. "In the name of the Father, The Son, and the Holy Spirit, Amen."

I remained standing at the pew level, signaling the audience to seat themselves in the polished walnut benches. As they settled, it struck me once again how fortunate I was to be called as the senior pastor to such an established, respected house of worship. What a promotion from my previous charge, a mission start-up church that began in a rented school auditorium! Now, I was at The Hill.

I began with my favorite sermon, an unexpected exposition of the prodigal son story. I knew I needed to deliver something different from this familiar theme, guessing that some of the senior members of this church had heard this text addressed no less than thirty times. They knew the usual sermon by heart: A call to acknowledge that God is the loving father. Getting right with God requires us to come to our senses and acknowledge our sins. The loving Father-God will always take us back, regardless of how bad we have been. I thought I would stir their minds with a new approach, asking them at the end to consider the question the parable begs: "Which son are you?" I was pleased with the delivery. I felt it was well received.

Grinning to myself, I take another sip, lost in reminiscence.

Early in the process of being introduced to The Hill, I was fortunate to meet Bonnie, a member of the search committee. She filled me in on the street version of my inaugural. She operated The Chat and Curl Salon. The following Monday afternoon, she had been giving seventy-six-year-old Maggie Johnsen her weekly wash and curl. Bonnie was pinning Maggie's hair when Maggie began her usual blunt banter with her life-long friend, Lizzie Thornton, seated in the chair to her right, waiting for her turn for a wash.

"So, Lizzie, what do you think of our new preacher?"

"Impressive, Maggie. Seemed to be a good speaker. And he didn't use any notes. I had no trouble hearing what he said. He didn't mumble his words, thank God!"

"I agree. But what about what he said? His take on the prodigal son?"

"That was a new twist I've never heard. Wasn't what I expected. Still thinking about it."

"I do wish he would use the pulpit. I'm not used to my minister being at eye level."

"I wish he would wear socks!"

"Do you think he will last?"

"We'll just have to wait and see, won't we?"

I like Bonnie. She has not only become a good friend over the past seven years, she is also a treasured source for feedback.

Enough memory lane. My empty cup reminds me I need to show up at the office before mid-morning.

CHAPTER TWO

M y dashboard clock reads 10:10 a.m. as I pull into my designated parking slot. I give myself another five minutes of solitude before opening the door. The past week was brutal. I glance in the rear view mirror and check myself. At least I remembered to shave. My eyes show fatigue, but no red spiders. I notice a few specks of grey invading my temple. How behaved I have become in my thirties. Was it that long ago in college that I had throbbing headaches every Monday? Those were the days I could do whatever I pleased on the weekends. As long as I showed up for classes and didn't embarrass the seminary, I was accountable to no one. I am really tired, but my fatigue this morning has nothing to do with substance abuse—it just comes with the job. I'll push through today.

I delay a few more moments and try to console myself regarding an ever-present tension as senior pastor of a county seat church. I am not an extrovert. Most of my colleagues are, however, or at least appear to be.

"I can be social," I tell myself, "but it is hard work. It drains me."

Days like yesterday, being around hordes of people, are a part of my job. I hope my inner struggles with this performance are not too obvious. But it does take its toll. Every fiber in my body feels rung out, no cordial greetings left in me. I hope today is quiet.

Frequently on Mondays, I remind myself of a principle I learned years ago from a pastor I admire. I had attended a gathering of other ministers, and Dr. William Self was the guest of honor. He expounded on his great success in building one of the fastest growing congregations in the Atlanta area. He also bragged about his management of weddings, officiating only if the bride and groom agreed that his sole involvement would be the fifteen-minute ceremony. As such, the minister of pastoral care conducted the pre-marriage counseling sessions. The associate pastor stood in for him at the rehearsal. He did not need to rehearse because he already knew what he was going to do and how to do it.

I boldly asked, "Dr. Self, you have shared with us your disciplined approach to ministry, how you construct your sermons, and running the business of the church like a CEO. It sounds like an exhausting task. When do you take time off?"

Dr. Self looked around the room and into the eager faces of those who wished to be as successful, then smiled. "I NEVER take Mondays off," he said, followed by a pregnant pause for effect, "because I never want to feel that bad on my own time."

As I open the car door and pull myself out, I am glad I adopted his policy on this Monday morning. The thought of my trip tomorrow into the Georgia foothills for trout fishing near my cabin, alone, gives a burst of energy to carry me through today.

As I enter the office suite, I half-heartedly greet Elizabeth the church administrator with the usual smile and "Good morning. How are you today?" but do not pause for an answer, instead heading straight to the office kitchen. I pour some brew into my favorite mug—hand-shaped pottery, glazed natural clay, with an exaggerated outline of a face featuring a long parsnip nose protruding under saggy, tired eyes—a joke gift from someone.

As I slide into my high-back desk chair, Elizabeth approaches with a bundle of pink "While You Were Away" message forms completed in her immaculate penmanship. She places them on my desk with a genuine, "Good morning, Brother Bobo," using my childhood name only allowed by my inner circle. She spends a few seconds rearranging the stack and, for emphasis, places her finger in the center of the top message. "You might want to address this one before you get too settled this morning. It is from Reggie Cornelius. He wants to see you. He didn't say so, but it sounded urgent."

CHAPTER THREE

As Elizabeth returns to her office area, and pulls the door closed behind her, I release a long, slow sigh. Reggie has been a frequent contact over the last few days and his need for attention is no surprise. His mother died last week after a long illness and her funeral yesterday was the largest The Hill has experienced in recent years. Actually, I thought the service went very smoothly. I retrieve from the corner of my desk the yet-to-be-filed order of service and my manuscript of the eulogy. *"Martha Grace Cornelius: A Grand Matron of The Hill and Nurturing Mother."* I smile. This eulogy has to be one of my best. I write a note on the upper margin of my manuscript: *Elizabeth, run spelling and grammar check then file in Dropbox Funerals folder for reprints as requested.*

Handling the pink slip with Reggie's number on it, I speculate on the urgency of the request. Surely, he does not need to complain about something in the memorial or graveside services. Bryan and the choir pulled off a miracle performance of Martha Grace's favorite hymn. Since she was a member of The Hill, I certainly don't expect an honorarium. However, she was also a very generous person and in her honor, I would not turn down a gesture of gratitude from her family. I have been waiting months for the funds to order that new set of Scripture Commentaries from Amazon. What could Reggie possibly need that is so urgent? Whatever it is, it can wait an hour or more for me to get my thoughts around the rest of this week, to sort out what I can do and what might need to wait.

I hear Elizabeth's voice on the phone intercom. "It's Reggie on line two, hoping to catch you before you leave to make hospital calls."

I suppress my groan, remind myself of my pastoral calling, and pick up the hand piece. "Good morning, Reggie, I was just about to call you. How are you today? It must be tough this morning to adjust to the big change in your life."

"Yes, it is a big adjustment, Pastor Jon. Last week was tough. You did a wonderful job yesterday. Couldn't have made it without your help and the church. It really made a difference." Reggie's voice sounds as tired as I feel. "I was really proud of my mother yesterday. Your description of her was so touching. She was indeed the most nurturing person I know. Thank you." He pauses a moment. "But the reality of life moving forward without her is sinking in quickly. I wondered if I might have a moment of your time today?"

"What about lunch, at Brubakers, say around 12:30?"

"Normally, that would be fine, Jon, but I need to see you privately. Could I meet with you at your office sometime today?"

"Sure," I reply as I scan my memory for conflicting obligations. "Let's make it at 2 p.m."

"See you then. Thanks, Pastor."

I put down the receiver and anxiety kicks up the juices in my empty stomach. Is this meeting about something I said in the eulogy? Did I make a mistake in a family name? Did I insult or overlook anybody? I force myself to be calm by admitting that I really do not know whether this urgent request for a meeting is good or bad news. Maybe it is good news! Maybe Miss Martha Grace has left the church a boatload of money in her will. Perhaps she made the church a beneficiary of a life insurance policy. Now there's a pleasant thought!

Thumbing again through the stack of pink slips, I pull out those that need immediate attention. Maggie has been admitted overnight at the hospital with tests to be run today. Bishop Carter wants to nominate me for a committee on stewardship. I leave the office with a short list of quick tasks that can be done around lunch.

After a brief visit with Maggie and husband George at Harris Memorial Hospital, and a call to the bishop to accept his invitation, I stop by Brubakers for my routine Monday lunch—quiche of the day, a cup of soup, and a small salad—then back to the office. Perhaps this meeting with Reggie will take pressure off the capital campaign for the Family Life Center addition.

By the time Reggie arrives, I am ready for two scenarios. I will accept responsibility for any mistakes in Martha's funeral yesterday and offer profound apologies. Or I will be surprised and gracious at an announcement of a windfall for the church.

I welcome him to my office and he quickly takes a seat in one of the paired wingback chairs. I settle into my overstuffed leather armchair. It makes me appear relaxed and accepting, something I learned in pastoral counseling classes years ago, and modeled after Dr. Self's own office layout.

"Pastor, I just want to reiterate what a fine job you did yesterday, and not only that, but also thank you for your wonderful care for Mother during her last few years in the nursing home and the last two weeks in intensive care…" He pauses, then adds with a tone of sadness, "…particularly your presence with us during the tough decision to remove life support. We really needed to bring an end to her suffering, and to ours as well…."

He chokes a bit on these last words and I am stirred as well. But I am also relieved to hear the praise. In my ten years of pastoring, I have become accustomed to such accolades. I know that pastoral care in the setting of hospice and bereavement is my spiritual gift. Shifting in my chair, to the subtle squeak of the leather, I prepare to receive the other possible cause for this visit.

I redirect the conversation to what I hope is a more positive topic. "Reggie, I suspect that you are now having to begin to address the issues around your mother's estate. She was always a very thoughtful and thorough lady, never to leave something undone or loose ends. She probably has everything in order, like she did for her funeral. Her details of what she wanted for her funeral were very helpful to us."

"Well, you're right, Pastor, but that's not why I'm here. I am now dealing with more immediate issues of our family legacy, which is why I needed to talk to you today. I need your pastoral advice on some matters."

I instantly process a private thought —*Amazon purchase of commentaries delayed again!*—and then respond.

"I'm glad to offer what advice might be helpful, but I have to acknowledge my limitations. So, how can I help you?"

"Father left a will when he died seven years ago, leaving his printing business to Mother and me. Mother thought that Dad's will regarding the business was sufficient for the both of them, so she never addressed that issue in her own will. You are very right on most parts, Pastor. She did indeed take great care to detail all the specifics of her personal belongings, right down to assigning every dish and piece of furniture. But she left the business ownership completely unchanged in her document."

Hearing Reggie's comments about wills raises my anxiety more than I expect. I remind myself I am not trained in legal opinion, and the last thing I want to do is get involved in a settlement of an estate. "Reggie, that is unfortunate that your mother made such an omission. I'm not an attorney. But it seems to me that if the company was willed to you and your mother by your father, his will would be sufficient. Have you consulted your attorney on this matter?"

"Yes, in fact, I spoke with him last week when I realized Mother was passing. And he suggested the same thing and promised to look into it. But Pastor, it's more complicated than Father's will."

CHAPTER FOUR

R eggie catches me glancing at the digital clock radio on the windowsill.

"Brother Jon, do you have just a few more minutes?" he pleads. "I really need to talk to someone about this."

I hear the stress in his voice and sense that a longer explanation is forthcoming. My afternoon plans dissolve.

"Of course, Reggie, that's what I am here for. Let me get us some coffee that we can sip while we chat. How do you take yours?"

"Thanks, Pastor. A cream and two sugars would be nice."

I elect not to call upon Elizabeth to bring us the beverages and interrupt the privacy of the conversation. Instead I excuse myself to retrieve the coffee for both of us. I use the task to think and to prepare for whatever might be coming. When I return with our two cups, Reggie is staring down at some spot between us on the blue Oriental rug spread out beneath our chairs.

He seems to reconnect with the present and begins with a surprise comment. "Pastor, your eulogy about Mother was something special. You seem to have had just the right words to describe her. I wonder if you might have a copy of what you said that I could keep. It would mean a lot to me."

"Absolutely. I'll arrange for that right away."

"Thanks again, Pastor, for letting me interrupt your afternoon. I don't want to bore you with all the details, but I believe it would be helpful for you to understand all that has happened as a result of Mother's death this week."

He scoots forward onto the front edge of the wingback, elbows on his knees, head leaning in toward me.

In a voice lower than the earlier conversation, he begins slowly. "I need to fill you in on some background. When I graduated from the Rochester Institute of Technology, I returned to help Father run our family printing business. You must remember my brother, Spike, you met him at Father's funeral. Anyway he had just finished boarding school in Macon. Spike's grades weren't so good, but he does have street smarts. He was a handful for my parents as a child, even more so during his teen years. Always the fun guy—setting off cherry bombs in the toilets in middle school and smoking pot behind the pizza joint. Spike didn't have a clue as to what he wanted to do. So, Father arranged for him to be admitted to Rochester, like he had arranged for me. And to Spike's credit, he went.

"But after the first year, he came home all cocky and arrogant. He said Rochester was the most boring town and the school was full of crazy teachers. He said he hated the printing business, always had, and would not go back."

Reggie takes a sip of coffee and continues.

"Of course, Father was crushed with disappointment because he wanted Cornelius Printing to be a family business. Father dreamed aloud of the day he would change the sign on the building to read *Cornelius & Sons Printing*.

"Nevertheless, he suggested Spike might go to another school and offered to pay whatever it took. Mind you, our parents were not well-educated. Father finished high school— tech school, actually—which had a printer's apprenticeship arrangement with the local union. Mother had just finished high school when they got married and she soon started raising a family. But they always held the value of a college education in high regard, which they felt they had missed. So, throughout our childhood years, they put away huge savings for our college education. That was what made it possible for me to attend Rochester. And my parents had made the same provision for Spike. Since I did not need all that was saved for me, my college saving plan was rolled over to Spike's, and it had grown to nearly $250,000."

He takes another sip of coffee. I am shocked by this amount, but try not to appear so. I match him with a sip myself.

"Reggie, that seems like a lot of money for a college fund."

"Yes, it is, actually. Instead of investing for retirement, our parents dedicated all of their savings to our education to help us get a good start. They thought they would work all their lives. Their idea of old age was to make sure we had that good start so we could take care of them. So, it was really more than just a college fund. It was also our "starting life fund.""

"So, back to Spike. He wanted the money from this account. He wanted to open a tattoo shop in the Dunwoody area north of Atlanta. He had picked up the tattooing skills on his own and had a few demonstrations on his inner forearm to show for it. Spike is very artistic. Although Father thought it was a bad idea, they struck a deal for him to move away to start his own business and live on his own terms."

Reggie pauses as though the admission of this inside family strife pains him to reveal to someone outside the family. Leaning back into the wings of the chair, he continues:

"In spite of the generous deal, Spike was very angry toward the family and the business. He said he didn't want any part of either;

that we were old fogies stuck in the fifties. He hurt my parents very badly, treated them cruelly.

"Spike was popping off one night in the backyard and cursing my parents, who were out of town, and we got into it. We had always tussled as kids, competing with each other over everything from the size of a candy bar to who sat in the front seat. I had always been afraid I could kill my brother with my bare hands—a swift knock of my fist on the side of his head, his fall striking his head on some brick and him dying. It always held me back until that night. But that night, with no parents around, we broke into an all-out fight. For twenty minutes or more, we wrangled and fought, spit and bit, to the point where we had bloody lips, loose teeth and eyes starting to swell shut. We were a mess. But I got the better of him, being the larger of us, and as we stood there shaking with our adrenalin depleting, we came to an agreement. He would take his sorry ass, his snotty arrogance, and disrespectful attitude toward our family and get out of town. And his reply was as deeply rooted, disavowing all ownership of the family. He was done with always being the kid of the Cornelius family who could never do anything right. He walked off that night and disappeared for several weeks.

"After about two months without any communication or contact, he shows up to get his stuff from his room and pins Father down about the money agreement. The next day, the two of them go off to the bank. Father hands him the cash in a suitcase, and armed with the conditions that Spike demanded, they part company. Father comes home, goes down to his woodshop in the basement and isolates himself for a week, depressed and crushed.

"We don't hear from Spike for several years. We hear *about* him, however. Bill collectors start calling my parents and even me, seeking his whereabouts. But we have no answers. Rumors surfaced occasionally that he had indeed opened a tattoo parlor in Marietta, that it had been raided by the Cobb County Sheriff and the Federal Alcohol, Tobacco and Firearms Bureau, but no arrests were made. Whatever word that *did* get back to us about Spike was always embarrassing.

"We heard that he got into drugs, had blown through all his money, and was in a rescue mission somewhere near Macon, and then to a mental health center over in Augusta for detox and rehab. He kept his distance all this time. I'll give him some credit. He never brought his shit—pardon my French, Pastor—home to our town. He kept his distance. And then, one day, about five years after he walked away from the bank and our father, he shows up. "What the hell?" I ask myself.

"Of course, Father is thrilled to see him. Mother breaks down in tears of relief that he is alive and in her arms. She wants him to stay and have a meal, 'Just like old times,' she says. He stays around as a guest in their house for several weeks. My parents call all excited that Spike has returned. It happens to be his birthday, and they want to have a party. So my wife and kids and I go over.

"Spike and I greet and embrace each other. I'm glad to see him, relieved that he is alive. I'm not immediately sure he is sober, but eventually I realize he is. He is a bit gaunt— scrawny, but clean. And we have a good dinner, with lots of his favorite food. Mother has baked his favorite cake. At first, I am uncomfortable and don't know what to make of this return. I'm a bit on edge, remembering the fight that night when we parted ways. But Spike is gracious and his pleasant demeanor begins to mellow my attitude towards him. We start talking about going fishing and hunting together again. However, it was obvious from the moment he showed up that he was unemployed, and broke.

"Next thing I know, Father creates a job for him at the printing business without my input. He later explained to me that 'we have to take care of family—that is what family is for.' I can't forget how Spike hated the printing business. At this point, I am now the CEO of Cornelius Printing, and the last thing I want is someone hanging around, drawing a salary in a business he hates. But Father, as the president of Cornelius, has the final word and Spike begins his return by cleaning the place from top to bottom.

"Admittedly, the place starts to shine with attention to corners and rooms that had long been neglected. Spike convinces Father that a new coat of paint on the inside and out would do wonders for the place and before a month passes, Spike is beginning to have an impact on our company. Even the pressmen like him, and they hang out together for smokes off the back loading dock. After a while, Father becomes convinced that he is showing some maturity and commitment to our family business and starts to give Spike more responsibility. Sometimes, Father does this with my input, and sometimes he just tells me that's the way it's going to be, and I have to accept it or cause a row in the family business.

"Four years go by, and Spike is head of production and thinks he knows every piece of equipment and every process in our business. He is into everything. He volunteers to go to every printing convention Father and I attend, and even adds some special seminars out of his own pocket. He really gets into the new stuff in the industry and starts exploring technology that sounds completely risky. Father kind of puts Spike in his place several times, explaining to him that the printing business is one of the most stable and unchanging industries in the business world. Modern businesses have always needed printing and always will. Father believes most of the stuff Spike is learning is just hype from the industry gurus who want to sound important.

"Cornelius Printing has been doing just fine for the past fifty years in Verona, Georgia, because we know our customers and they are loyal to us. No need to go off the deep end by buying the latest scanner, or plate processor. Ink on paper, in large volumes, at good prices, that is the name of the game in printing. Do it, do it right, and everything will be okay. So Spike just backs off. But he doesn't quit going to all those conferences and seminars. He just bides his time until Father passed away seven years ago, and then he starts making his pitch to me on how we should make some changes."

While I am listening to Reggie unwind this long tale, I am thinking to myself on another track. What is going on here? In my ten years of ministry, I have never heard such a long and unbroken description of someone's past with a family member. Usually, I need to pull stuff out of people to understand the problem, but this guy just goes on and on without any encouragement from me. My training starts to kick in, and I am guessing this whole sordid account with Spike from childish brother rivalry to today's crisis has been bottled up inside Reggie, and perhaps for the first time, it is spilling forth like a broken dam. I commit myself to listen and ride this monologue just to see where it will take us.

Reggie continues without missing a beat.

"At first, I am reluctant to change anything after Father dies. I want to keep everything running just the way he taught me. But eventually, I start to yield on a few areas and give Spike some money to experiment with some of his ideas. Half of them are busts, but the other half prove to make sense at some level, enough so that the good ideas actually outweigh the bad."

Reggie pauses to check his watch, which must convince him that he has plenty of time left.

"Brother Jon, I'm sure much of this is boring to you, and you're not interested in the technical part of the printing business, so I'll cut to the chase. Over the past ten years, Cornelius Printing has been through a lot of changes and survived the big recession of 2008. We are okay now, looks like we are going to survive. Here's the point of what I need to talk to you about."

Finally, I whisper inside my brain. Reggie perches again on the edge of his seat, looking straight into my eyes, and with a lowered, calmer, all-business voice, he continues.

"A major printing conglomeration has approached me and wants to buy me out. They have been talking to me privately for six months, but I have been putting them off because of Mother's condition and the need to have her involved in the decision, since she and I shared ownership of the company. I expected that she would not live much longer and that I would make my decision about this offer after she passed.

"Well, Pastor, two things have happened in the past few weeks that have put a tremendous amount of pressure on me, so much so that I cannot sleep at night for stressing over it. First, the big guys who want to buy me out have been keeping tabs on Mother's condition and didn't want to push me too hard for a decision while she was in such sad shape. But, along with a huge flower spray for her funeral, they sent word last week when she died, that they wanted to move quickly with their offer. In a separate letter, they explained they had several companies in mind to purchase, but only had resources for buying a limited number, and Cornelius was one of their top choices. They seemed a bit pushy, considering the timing of Mother's funeral, but explained that they needed to make their decision—or rather, I needed to make my decision to accept or pass on their offer within the next forty-five days or the offer would be off the table. I hadn't planned to have to make such a decision so fast, and I'm in a bit of shock presently."

Reggie takes a deep breath and continues without giving me time to respond.

"Now what has further complicated this situation is the fact that Spike has somehow gotten wind of this offer, even though he is not an owner of the company. He wants in on the decision to sell, to which he has no legal right, but more importantly, he is claiming he has a right to some of the sale price if I sell. He claims the family owes him a share of the proceeds.

"That's why I went into such detail about his leaving and then coming back. Nowhere along the way did our parents ever acknowledge that he had any right to the company. As far as I'm concerned," —he pounds his fist on the arm of the chair— "he clearly gave up all rights to Cornelius Printing fifteen years ago in the backyard when we had that fight. I also believe he took his share of the family's estate when he walked away from Father at the bank, with three hundred thousand dollars in cash in his suitcase. But he sees it differently. He thinks—at least what he told me late last night when he confronted me with the rumor that Cornelius might be for sale—he is due a huge chunk of the profit from the sale of the business. He claims he is responsible for making it a viable business. I don't think so, and I told him so in no uncertain terms.

"So this morning, he called me before daybreak and told me I needed to carefully consider my actions regarding the sale. If I didn't include him in the negotiation, and I didn't include him in getting his fair share, he would seek a court injunction against the sale and find an attorney to help him fight for his rights. If he does that, Pastor, and this is what I explained to him, he will jeopardize the offer. The big guys don't have time to fool around with family squabbles over businesses like ours. There are hundreds of other companies they can purchase without our hassles."

For the first time, Reggie invites a response. "Pastor Jon, what do I do?"

"Reggie, I can understand how all this could be very stressful for you at this time. I can only imagine the feelings that must be going through you, particularly so close to your mother's death last week. You are right, this is complicated."

I pause for a moment, reach for my cold cup and take a short sip to gather my thoughts and assess my footing for what I will say next. "Would you like a warm-up on your coffee, Reggie? Mine's gone cold. Let me get you a refill," I offer as I make my way to the coffee station next to my writing desk. Upon my return, I top off each cup and set the carafe on a magazine lying on the lamp table. Sitting on the edge of my seat and leaning forward, I carefully phrase my words.

"Reggie, I thank you for sharing this information with me. I know it is heavy on your heart. In a moment, I want to offer a prayer for you, but before I do, I need some help from you to understand a few things. What are you most concerned about regarding this information that you have just shared with me?"

Reggie takes his time to respond, perhaps partly to reflect on his answer, or to simply recover from exhaustion. I suspect he feels like he has just let all the air out of his soul.

"Good question, Pastor." He sips from his coffee mug, which he has wrapped both hands around. "I'm fearful about several things. One is my retirement that I have been working toward for the past fifteen years. A sale like this is just what I had planned on. I fear my plans may be in serious jeopardy now that Spike is involved. Another concern I have is that if Spike gets his back up, if he actually moves forward with legal action, our family issues are going to become public and spread all over town. It could get ugly."

"I understand," I reply. "It sounds like a lot of this is a matter of estates, and wills, and business deals. So, I'm curious with how you see my role in this. I don't know anything about estates, or wills, and I am definitely weak on business matters. That is why I rely on people like you as trustees for the church—to keep our church, and me, out of trouble."

"Yeah, you're right about that, Pastor. You are clueless sometimes about the reality of business, always looking at problems as though they can be settled with prayer or faith or just believing the right things." He grins widely to indicate he is jabbing me with his dry humor.

"But you got me to thinking about this a few Sundays ago when you preached a sermon about that guy who went to Jesus and asked him to make his brother settle his estate with him. I think I'm right about that scripture reading. Anyway, I don't recall what your sermon was about that day. Sorry. But the reading never left my mind. So, when this matter came up about me and Spike, I thought the place to start would be with you. What advice do you have to offer?"

"Yes, Reggie, I remember that reading. The text that day was from Luke, I think, the twelfth chapter. I remember reading that passage and thinking it was a bit of a challenge for me, glad at the time that I was doing a series from the Epistle readings of Colossians. What are your thoughts about that dialogue of the brother with Jesus?"

"I don't know. That's why I came to you."

CHAPTER FIVE

Thirty minutes after Reggie leaves our session to return to his business, I return three calls pressed upon me by Elizabeth. It is now mid-afternoon, and I realize my plans for the afternoon have been totally wrecked. I had hoped to get in about three hours of research on my doctoral studies. I mumble to myself that this attempt to stretch me academically might be foolhardy and grandiose. Obligations are pulling at me in every direction. What was I thinking, volunteering myself for this advanced degree?

I rub the pink callback slip naming my project consultant and ponder whether to make the call to Dr. Dan this afternoon or wait until tomorrow. He usually tries to connect with his students on Mondays and I know I need to touch base on our progress toward a selection for a final ministry project. But I am stuck, and have no idea where to go with this, so calling him back this afternoon will just underscore that procrastination has once again gotten the best of me. If I wait until tomorrow, there is a good chance that Dr. Dan will not be available because of his teaching schedule at the seminary. If I leave a message on the voice mail on a busy Tuesday, I can feign an attempt to connect for this week, and postpone for another seven days the dreaded discussion.

If only I could just skip ahead to the end: The Reverend Doctor

Jonathan Amos Boatwright. It sounds so much better than Jambo, a name that has followed me through childhood as a military brat. Formally, I prefer to be addressed as Jonathan, without the Reverend part. I hate the title "Reverend." It seems so off-putting. Frankly, I don't like being reverent most of the time, and really don't like trying to live up to the idea that I am somehow supposed to exhibit a certain demeanor in professional life which places me in a status that is holier than average. To be thought of as more spiritually focused is okay, but not more reverent.

Why did I pressure myself to go after this Doctor of Ministry thing anyhow? Admittedly, my return to the campus during the special DMin sessions in January, June and July were enjoyable. Those two-week sessions whetted my appetite for greater learning and a chance to be around studious people who wrestled honestly with the questions of faith, scripture and church politics. And the continuing online sessions and chat room banter for the weeks following each on-campus session have forced me to continue digging for answers for my own journey in faith.

As I drive toward my suburban home five miles away, I continue to ponder my decision to enter the DMin program and my commitment to continue. Now that I have completed the classwork and engaged with other students and professors, I must now launch the final push for the big project. I have heard from other colleagues and some of my former Master of Divinity classmates at Westminster Seminary that the toughest part of the DMin is yet to come—the infernal project. I have also been sobered by learning that about one-third of those accepted and beginning the DMin drop out because they cannot buckle down and do the work required for that project. When I heard about this high attrition rate, I vowed that I would never quit. But lately, I have been entertaining some doubts about the sanity of that earlier commitment. *Why am I doing this to myself, my family, my church? Why am I stretching myself so thin? Isn't there enough to do, enough sermons to prepare, classes to teach, committee meetings to attend, hospital visits to make, and funerals to serve? Why do I need to add this burden?*

I turn and drive between the curved stone walls identifying the entrance of the Assisi Estates then start down Walden Boulevard. The upper-middle-class status of my neighborhood reminds me that part of my pursuit of the DMin has to do with my search for recognition and status, something I do not readily admit to anyone other than my clinical pastoral education supervisor, whom I have not seen in several years. Waving to Emily and Duane Nicholson taking their late afternoon stroll down the sidewalk, I remember my conversation with Uncle Clarence, my mother's brother.

Uncle Clarence was the star of my mother's siblings, a minister in Valdosta, the first male of the Gordon family line to finish high school and complete a college degree. The Gordon clan held him in even higher regard when he finished seminary with a Masters in Divinity. His oldest sister, my mother, could not contain her pride when she watched him, at the age of thirty, hooded with the colors as he received his Doctor of Ministry degree at Vanderbilt. I turn down Tuscany Drive toward our house and remember fondly my conversation with Uncle Clarence about why he had chosen to be different than the rest of his family. Why had he entered the ministry, elected to wear a robe in the pulpit when no other Baptist preacher in town did the same, *and* pursued a Doctor of Ministry? Uncle Clarence grinned when he explained the real reason for all these differences.

"Jambo, it is simply my way of getting the lint out of my hair."

When I responded with a puzzled look, Clarence went on to explain how he and my mother had grown up in a large family in Thomaston, Georgia.

"As early as my sophomore year in high school, I started working part-time in the textile mills, alongside my father and mother, and a dozen uncles, cousins and aunts. It was what you did if you lived in Thomaston. And if you had a chance to go into Atlanta for a Braves game, you had to be careful when you got ready to leave town that you had cleaned yourself so thoroughly that there was no trace that you worked in the mills. People always ridiculed mill workers when they went into places like Atlanta, or downtown Macon. They were called lint-heads because it was often obvious from the fuzz in their hair that they worked in the mills.

"So," Clarence explained to me, "I have to admit that the robe and the DMin helps me get the lint out of my hair."

I pull into our driveway and push the button on the visor to open the garage door. While waiting for enough room to get in, I reflect on my own choice for entering the DMin from the Conley School of Theology at Epworth University. It isn't to get the lint out of my hair. It is a way to get the brass off my shoulder and put doctoral stripes on my sleeve. It was to ease the memory of the years of my childhood as an Army brat, the child of a non-commissioned officer, an enlisted sergeant, moving about every eighteen to twenty-four months from one base to another. We had just enough time at one school to learn who I could trust as a friend before being shipped abruptly a thousand miles away to catch up with Dad at his new post assignment. Those were days of constant rootlessness, learning to lean on myself, never committing to people or school or community because they were always temporary. And so was I.

I watched Dad put in twenty-five years of being caught between pleasing the officer over him and placating the enlisted soldiers under him, counting the years, biding his time until he could retire with a small pension and stop moving. I wanted something more.

As the garage door closes behind me, the lights in the garage remind me that I am surrounded by a home that has been my daily landing spot for the past seven years. I am pleased with my choices. The DMin is my way of saying I am different. I am going to push as far and as high as I can go because I can, and I owe it to myself and my family not to leave a stone unturned—to be the best I can be at what I do! Abandoning the DMin is not an option! Case closed!

I pass through the kitchen and peck Marsha on the cheek, dip my finger in the chili pot, lick it with approval, and confirm that I have about an hour before dinner—enough time to mow the yard.

Mowing is something I never mind. A large span of manicured grass is more pleasure than work. It measures in some manner the distance between this suburban home and the military posts, where there was no home ownership, and the grass, if there was any, belonged to the compound. I confess; I get into mowing—the 3M headset muffling the roar of the Briggs and Stratton engine. The finished piece of artwork, observed during sundown while sipping an Arnold Palmer, is pastoral, in the literal sense. I like mowing because right away, my work and effort produce visible results. I can see where I have been, and where I have yet to go. There is evidence of hard work.

Such evidence is seldom present in ministry. I can work my ass off, bearing down at the task from sun-up to sundown, and sometimes through the night. Yet at the end of the week or month or annual report to the board or congregation, I actually have very little to show for it. Yeah, souls were "saved," baptisms were carried out, weddings performed, funerals conducted. Lots of activity, but is anything really different? Grass cutting is different immediately, if not for long.

Mowing the grass is also a venue for processing thoughts and feelings. If I have a bad run-in with one of the deacons over some matter that seems trivial to one and an absolute to the other, I can work out my stress without damage to my reverend status. Sometimes, I will name the dandelions after the very characters in my ministry who cause my blood pressure to rise, and then take delight in seeing blossoms and stems cut into a thousand pieces and discharged out the side chute of the mower. But not tonight.

On the agenda for tonight's mowing is the matter of the DMin project. Several areas might prove helpful to the congregation I serve, and other areas might be more helpful in my future career opportunities. Following the walk-a-long mower, I ponder the options: I could develop a project around worship. Or a capital campaign for the family life center—discussed for years but never got past the strategic, long-range planning phase. Maybe I could choose a more academic subject, something that could be transferred to other disciplines and broaden my influence in the denomination—such as foreign mission strategies using local congregations, or a stewardship campaign design and development.

As I round the lawn the third time, I admit in the space between my ear protectors that I really don't have the heart for any of these subjects. What I need is something about which I can be passionate, excited; something out of the ordinary that stretches me beyond my comfort zone. But as the area of uncut grass becomes smaller and smaller, I realize that I need to be reasonable. If I go too far afield, I will have a tough time getting approval from the DMin Director. And I don't want to set myself up for a project so out of my realm that it requires totally new research and a greater workload.

What if I could find some area that I do frequently and simply expand on that, perfecting something I am already good at? What is it that I enjoy, that I can simply do more of and not become fatigued? Or better yet, what area can I study that will make my life easier? What is my most difficult, most challenging area presently? Funerals! Yes, funerals. I seem to have a lot of them—about six a month, I guess. For sure, my funeral routine is beginning to get stale and somewhat routine by virtue of the frequent demand, but my parishioners always seem so appreciative of what I do. And I also have caught the attention of both funeral homes in town, becoming their go-to preacher when a family does not have a local minister.

Yes, funerals: the preparation for the event—from the time of a terminal diagnosis, to the details of the customized funeral service, to the follow-up with bereavement counseling. Funerals it is! And the grass is now smooth, another masterpiece at 6312 Tuscany Drive.

After a chili dinner with cornbread and jalapeños, and a dollop of Lizzie's homemade chow-chow, I load the dishwasher, clear up the pots and pans, put away the leftovers, and polish the granite counter-top. Meanwhile, my son Rusty completes his eighth-grade homework assignment, daughter Priscilla practices for her piano lesson, and my spouse Marsha chills with a chardonnay and watches her favorites compete on a televised talent show.

With renewed dedication to the DMin and with less than one year left in a three-year window, I enter my paneled private study just off the formal living room. There I settle into my favorite reading chair and rest my legs on the ottoman. I pull from the side table a leather-covered tablet holder and grab my favorite fountain pen, a black ceramic Waterman. It is almost a talisman of my renewed spirit, the first of many in my pen collection. This one was a gift from a parishioner who was grateful for the funeral I led for their twenty-one-year-old son. It was my first funeral, and a tough one: suicide—with a shotgun. Messy. Rolling the Waterman between my finger and thumb, I remember being totally unprepared, yet surviving the graveside and small family gathering, noting the grateful but deeply bereaved parents.

There have been at least three hundred funerals since then. I keep a log of them in my Pastor's Manual. I am now on Volume IV. I open it to the first blank page and enter a summary of the record of Martha Grace Meeks Cornelius, Date June 22, 2011. Address: 1776 Maple Drive, Verona, GA. Church Membership: The Hill Church. Place of Service: The Hill Church. Interment: Overview Cemetery, Verona, GA. Remarks: A life-long faithful member of the church she loved. I pause for a moment then thumb back through the funeral records, and find in the back of the second volume the information for Mr. Jack A. Cornelius. Date: June 1, 2004. Address: 1776 Maple Drive, Verona, GA. Church Membership: The Hill Church. Place of Service: The Hill Church. Interment: Overview Cemetery, Verona, GA. Remarks: A standard bearer in The Hill Church.

I hold the record book open on my lap for several minutes and recall that service. It was very near the beginning of my tenure with the church. In my first two months here, I had taken note of this tall, thin man on the third row to my left, never smiling, never singing, but in regular eye contact with me, particularly during the sermons, as though Mr. Cornelius was taking in every word carefully. On a Monday morning, I received a phone call from a member that Jack Cornelius had been taken to the hospital Sunday afternoon and was in intensive care. I realized quickly that I had yet to carry out my introductory visit to Mr. Cornelius and was a bit anxious upon arrival at the intensive care unit, unclear about the identity of the family members. After the round of introductions to Mrs. Cornelius, her two sons, Reggie and Spiro, and their wives, Bonnie and Melissa, the family shared that Jack had suddenly doubled over in abdominal pain mid-afternoon the previous day. He was rushed to the emergency room at Harris Memorial and then immediately taken to intensive care, where he remained semi-conscious and heavily drugged with pain medications. His wife and sons had been awaiting word from the doctor.

Reggie, who had been on the committee that called me to The Hill, filled me in on who was related to whom, and how his father, Jack, was the founder and president of Cornelius Printing, the place that also printed the order of worship and weekly newsletters for The Hill. Within the hour, a short, middle-aged man dressed in green scrubs entered the room, and all voices fell silent as he peered through his wire frames, then moved to stand directly in front of Mrs. Cornelius, who was seated. He was the family surgeon and had conducted several operations on one family member or another. Grace remained seated as her two sons rose from theirs to stand on either side of the surgeon, whose face was grave. He held out his hand to her and as they clasped, he spoke quietly.

"Grace, your husband is very ill, as you might expect. We are still trying to determine what is happening, and we don't have a diagnosis yet. We are waiting on the results of his blood work and some reports back from some specialists I've brought in on his case. Right now, his condition is touch-and-go. I'm going to let you in, one family member at time, to see him for just a few minutes apiece. He is asking for you. I know this is hard, but try not to upset him. Stay calm and positive. He needs your support, but he doesn't need any excitement. The nurse will be back in a few minutes and will take you back. I'll be in touch as soon as we learn something."

And then he slipped away down the hall before anyone could ask any questions.

When the nurse came to the door and called out, "Cornelius family," the mother, her two sons, and I rose together and followed the nurse to the entrance of the intensive care waiting room. I remember holding back so as not to intrude, since I was not family, but Reggie grabbed me by the coat sleeve and pulled me along. "We're probably going to need you, Pastor."

I recall standing just outside his intensive care room, looking through the plate glass window at Jack connected to wires, three tubes, and a small oxygen mask over his nose and mouth. Grace went in first, with Reggie by her side to support her. Spiro stood leaning against the outer doorframe, waiting his turn. I looked around the unit, getting my bearings for future reference, as I expected more visits with other parishioners in this ICU would be forthcoming. When Reggie and his mother left the room, Spiro went in for several minutes, then exited. Reggie then re-entered and remained by his father's bedside for ten minutes or more. When he came out, he looked at me and said, "Father wants to see you for a few minutes."

I entered and slowly approached Jack's bedside, and connected more intensely with the same eyes I had seen from the pulpit just a day before. Jack's eyes telegraphed pain and fear as his hands gripped mine.

"Pastor, thank you for being here. I want you to know that I really like you. I think you are a great pastor and a sound preacher. I don't know what is happening to me, but I'm a bit fearful, not for myself, but for my wife. She is somewhat of a helpless creature, and I don't know what she will do without me. Will you pray for me, and pray for her?"

So, I did, with carefully chosen words that expressed divine care, but also sensitivity to what I—as their new pastor—did not really know about the family at that point, including details about Jack's health.

That Tuesday evening, after dinner with my family, I made a quiet trip back to the hospital to see how the family was coping. Upon arrival, I found Reggie and Grace huddled together in the corner of the intensive care waiting room. They shared the news of the diagnosis—inoperable and advanced pancreatic cancer, which was causing severe internal bleeding. The prognosis did not look good, so the nursing staff was allowing longer visits at Jack's bedside, provided there was minimal conversation. Spiro was taking the current shift. I spent about two hours with them as each family member rotated to Jack's bedside in twenty-minute shifts, before finally making my own visit. I offered a softly spoken recitation of the Twenty-Third Psalm and a very brief prayer for peace and comfort.

Early the next morning, I got the call from Reggie that Jack had just passed away. Reggie asked me to come to Grace's home to be with the family and make arrangements for the funeral, which I did. It was in the preparation of that funeral that I began to learn the differences between Reginald Abbott Cornelius, and his younger brother, Spiro Kenan Cornelius—better known to the family and the community as "Spike."

That contrast became apparent immediately with regard to which ministers should be included in the service. It is not uncommon in North Georgia to have two or more ministers performing some role in a service. In the case of Jack's funeral, I quickly realized that my predecessor, Rev. Jack Harmon, had been the pastor for Grace and Jack for twenty years before retiring and moving to Clemson to be near his daughter. If Reverend Harmon was available, it only made sense to invite him to offer the eulogy. Frankly, I was relieved that someone with a relationship with Jack longer than my brief two months was able to comfort the family and church at this loss of such a prominent member.

Of course, Reggie wanted me to conduct the service. However, Spike would not be satisfied until his own pastor, Brother Rusty Cognac, had a part.

"After all," Spike argued, "the pastor's role at a funeral is to minister to the members of his flock. Rusty is my pastor, has been for the past four years since I joined the Holy Trinity Community Church." Spike reminded his brother and mother, and informed me, in a sarcastic tone, "It is Brother Rusty, not Rev. Harmon, and it is Holy Forgiveness, not The Hill, that led me to the Lord and got me saved and away from the chain of alcohol."

Who could argue against such rationale at such a time as this?

Twirling the Waterman between my fingers, my memory deepens. That was not the only thing Spike demanded. I had worked closely with Bryan, the organist and choirmaster at The Hill, to make sure the choir was robed, rehearsed and in full presentation for this funeral. Between the two of us, we had selected "How Firm a Foundation" as a congregational hymn to be sung during the procession. "How Great Thou Art" would be the choir anthem immediately after the procession—a classic piece which made full use of the 30-rank organ with it's new digital processor that perfectly mimicked the sound of a genuine pipe organ.

I smile as I remember my comeuppance when I presented the program outline to the family on Friday afternoon. Spike immediately expressed dissatisfaction with the production, saying it sounded more like a dirge than a celebration of life. He wanted the service to be more evangelistic, with the singing of "I'll Fly Away" first, accompanied by the praise band from Holy Forgiveness, then joined in by the entire congregation with a big finale at the end. To keep peace in the family at such a crucial moment, we accepted Spike's suggestion, which left Bryan and me to manage some semblance of our sense of worship decorum appropriate for The Hill.

By the time the service was over, Jack Cornelius had been lifted up to Heaven with an eulogy that caused some to not recognize its subject, followed by a soul-searching, Hell-threatening sermon on getting your soul set right with God by confessing Jesus as your Lord and Savior. It also included an impromptu altar call by Brother Rusty, cajoling his worship band to break out in multiple verses of "Just As I Am!" and a finale recession of drums, banjos, and electric guitar to counterbalance the organ prelude an hour and a half earlier.

I carefully place the beloved Waterman back into its desktop cradle and close the covers of the Funeral Record book. I realize the patriarch funeral seven years ago was a window into much of what was currently at stake in the Cornelius family, with the passing of its matriarch and the funeral of Grace Cornelius. It left the estate uncertain between two sons, sons as different as night and day.

CHAPTER SIX

"Hello, this is Dr. Dan," is the surprise of the day for me when I call my project consultant.

"Uh, hello, is this Dr. Dan?" I stutter into the receiver.

"Yes, who is this?" replies the voice on the other end.

"Oh, Dr. Dan, I didn't expect you to be available at this hour and was going to leave you a message. This is Jonathan Boatwright. Good morning."

"Yes, Jonathan, I'm glad we connected. I've been meaning to talk to you for a while now. I'm right between classes at this moment, but we do need to talk. Let's reconnect at 11:15, after my last morning class. We need to set up a time to meet. Give me a call then."

I continue to hold the receiver as Dr. Dan hangs up. I feel a thud in my gut as I cradle the receiver. This is not going as planned. I was going to call Dr. Dan during class time, knowing he was teaching, leave a message that I was returning his call, apologize for missing him, and then end with some innocuous commitment about trying to reach each other before the end of the week. But my ducking has just been short-circuited. Dr. Dan's voice sounded like it was on the edge of guarded irritation.

I press the intercom and dial my assistant in the next room. "Elizabeth, please remind me to make a call at 11:15 this morning to Dr. Dan at Epworth. It's very important. Thanks."

For the next couple hours, I try to concentrate on the lectionary reading for two Sundays away. Seven months ago, during my planning retreat at the lake, I laid out my sermon series for the summer in order to guide Bryan in worship planning, which includes the music as well as the children's sermon. This particular Sunday is at the end of that planning session, when I was running out of time on the lake. I recall just dashing down the readings and leaving the subject summary and the title with the deadly three letters "TB-D"—"to be determined." Now it is crunch time. The readings have been predetermined by the lectionary, and Bryan can build a general worship program around that information. But Elizabeth needs the sermon title to draft the printed order of worship before the Monday morning deadline. I stare for several minutes at the scriptural references, and my notes:

> 2 Samuel 5:2-5, 9-10 …*David brings ark to Jerusalem…gets carried away in worship with wild dancing, embarrasses King Saul's family…*

> Amos 1:1, 7:10-14 (alternative) …*the plumb line … threat to the king… not a prophet but a herdsman, a dresser of sycamore trees.*

> Ephesians 1:3-14 …*in Christ …an inheritance…*

> Mark 6:14-29 …*beheading of John the Baptist…*

For each reading, I can imagine some vague launching point for a sermon theme, but it leaves me empty. It is the middle of July, and I expect a very low attendance. The few who will attend on a mid-summer Sunday either have no other place to go because they are too old, or too poor. Or they might be antsy, itching to get through an obligation to attend services and anxious to head to the lake for an afternoon of water skiing and sunset barbeques.

I search again for a possible focus text, but my mind migrates to the thud in my gut. I am dreading the call I must make at 11:15 a.m. I know what the call will be about—what is the DMin project?—and I am not ready to discuss it.

Elizabeth's voice on the desk intercom ends my morning drudgery with a reminder to place my call to Dr. Dan.

"Dr. Dan, this in Jonathan Boatwright. I'm glad we finally connected. Sorry to have missed your call last week, but it was quite hectic. We had a major funeral, which, as you know, can throw a week's plan completely off-track. What did you need to talk about?"

"Jonathan, thanks for calling me back. Yeah, I remember those days as a pastor and how those unplanned crises can set you back. Jonathan, I need a summary of your project proposal in four weeks and have not heard from you since we last met at the project workweek back in March. Are you making any progress?"

"Yes, in fact. Just this weekend, I began to think about a subject that I might develop. I want to focus on funerals. Seems I've had a lot of them since I moved to this church, and it's an area where I can see room for improvement."

"Tell me more," Dr. Dan replies.

"Well, it's something I think I can get my hands around and do a good job. I was thinking about analyzing the funerals I have conducted for the past ten years, looking for where things went exceptionally well on my part, and also identifying the places where I seemed to bomb, at least to me. Well... maybe not bombed, but just felt it was less than my best. From there, I would develop some insight with further reading of resources on how I might develop a systematic approach to the preparation of funerals. This would help me to make better use of my time. This last week, I realized how much time I spend just getting geared up for each funeral. If I could set up my own system of approach, I could condense that prep time and maybe do a better job. In short, by perfecting a method for funeral preparation, I could get better at it and lower my stress."

I wait for a response to the junk that is now just flying out of my head, having not given funerals serious thought since three days ago behind the lawn mower. I grin to myself for my quickness, then shift to anxiety, waiting several seconds before Dr. Dan replies.

"Jonathan, pardon the pun, but, to me," he pauses, "the subject of funerals sounds like a big dead end. I think you might be wasting your time on this subject. I have already reviewed your funeral materials from assignments, and I think you have a better than average handle on that subject. You need something that stretches you, pulls you into an area you have not delved into before."

"Oh, I'm sorry you're disappointed. I thought it was a good idea," I reply, for a lack of a more thoughtful reaction.

"Jonathan, it's been a while since we've met together. Why don't you come down to the campus this Friday? We can meet and go over some other project ideas that might work for you. Are you available?"

"Sure, Dr. Dan, I think I can work that out. What's a good time for you?"

"Let's do it over lunch, Friday. Meet me in my office just before noon and we can go off campus for a sandwich. See you then, Jonathan. Gotta go. Bye."

Holding the receiver against my chest, I slide down into my chair, deflated. My project consultant has just called me out diplomatically for what we both know is nonsense. I hang up the phone, walk out of the office without a word to anybody, get in my car and drive silently four blocks away to the NuWay stand. Two all-the-way deluxe chili dogs with French fries and a large Coke is the order. I hereby postpone my commitment to a low-fat diet until Wednesday.

CHAPTER SEVEN

"**B**rother Jonathan," I hear over my left shoulder and then feel the touch of a palm there. It's Spike, smiling and extending his hand. I wipe my right one clean of the chili and cheese drippings and greet him with a firm handshake.

"Spike, nice to see you. You getting yourself a mid-week hot dog fix?"

"Yeah, it helps get over hump day. I just wanted to say thank you for Mom's service. I appreciate all you did."

"Why, thank you, Spike. That means a lot to me. You eating alone today? Please join me."

"Think I will…Ma'am, I'll get what Brother Jonathan just ordered."

Spike takes the counter swivel stool to my right. Immediately, I notice Spike's left arm is covered from his short shirt sleeve to his wrist with tattoos. I don't want to stare, but my eyes cannot escape the bright blues, yellows, and reds, intermixed with the typical faded black patterns. I quickly check this behavior and look into Spike's bright blue eyes.

"Like I said before, that was some service, Brother Jonathan, some service. A great send-off for Mom. She suffered a long time before the end, but all the music and wonderful things people said about her helped us forget all that. It's been a while since I was in that church, and I was surprised at how friendly the people were to me and my family. They really loved my mom."

"Yes, Spike, that service was a genuine expression of how much they loved your mother. She was a great lady, a good Christian."

"Brother Jonathan, thank you for letting my pastor have a part. I know it was not what The Hill is used to, no offense, but it meant a lot to me that he was involved. He has a way of speaking that touches my heart."

"No offense taken, Spike. That's what funerals are supposed to do—help us celebrate a life, to comfort each other and to praise God. I think we did a great job of getting all that done. You agree?"

"Indeed."

"So, how's the printing business going this summer? I'm sure the plant had a bit of disruption with the funeral and all. I think I saw a lot of your employees at the service and reception."

"Yes, that's all part of a family business," Spike continues as the waitress plops down his order in front of him. Instinctively, Spike bows his head for several seconds before attacking his meal as though it was about to leave his plate on its own.

After he swallows his first mouthful, followed by a big gulp of Coke, he continues. "At the shop, we like to think we're all family, even if their last name is not Cornelius. We watch out for one another, just like Mom and Dad did when they first started it a long time ago. What about those Falcons at the summer camp workouts this week? Do you think the new coach will switch quarterbacks this season?"

I rack my brain for a response to this abrupt change in topic. "Hard to tell at this point," I reply. It is my only answer to guard the truth—I have little or no interest in professional football, except as it conflicts with attendance on Sundays when the Falcons play at 1 p.m. For the rest of that fast meal, I nod as Spike pontificates with predictions of wins and losses for each game of the upcoming NFL season.

Traveling between hospitals and visiting a nursing home later, I reflect on the brief encounter with Spike. I know very little about Reggie's brother and am ashamed to have formed some opinions of Spike based solely on Reggie's description. Perhaps that is not fair to Spike. I return to the office for a final update and acknowledge Elizabeth's stern reminder that she is still waiting on my sermon title and text for Sunday next, which I promise for first thing tomorrow morning. I quickly scan the desktop calendar, check for any issues that might challenge that promise, and then head home for dinner. It is rush "moment" in the small suburb of Verona, so I use the long red light to place a call.

"Reggie, this is Jonathan. Are you free for breakfast in the morning? You've been on my mind a good bit since we last talked, and I want to touch base with you again. …Okay, seven sharp at Frank's. I'll save a booth for us in the back. See you then."

CHAPTER EIGHT

Near daybreak, I slip quietly into my study and give serious thought to my sermon plans for the remainder of the summer, at least until Labor Day. I flow through the process and complete the forms the staff will use to coordinate the remaining details. Next, I commit myself to the first week of September for my semi-annual retreat for sermon and worship planning. At the end of the worship form, I post a sticky note to Elizabeth: *E, please contact Edward Malcom and reserve his lake cabin again for me for September 8-13, if it is available. Thxs, JMBo.*

Dropping the form on Elizabeth's vacant desk, I hurry off to Frank's to get my favorite seat—right side, all the way in the back. After Reggie arrives, we both place our orders for "the usual" with our favorite server, Ethel, and I begin the conversation.

"Reggie, the first thing I'd like to say is that I'm honored to be your pastor, and even more so that you brought me your concerns about your business and what's at stake with you right now. I can't say I understand all that is taking place, but I want to learn more. Can you tell me more?"

"Pastor Jon, I have to admit I was a bit hesitant to bring this to you. You don't seem to be the business type, and I was afraid you might just dismiss me with some prayer and wish me the best. Thanks for following up. What more would you like to know?"

Cooling my coffee with a spoon, I pause to think what information could be useful. Speaking softly, so as not to be overheard in the next booth, I respond, "I would like to hear more about the potential sale of your business and how it will affect your life. Are you planning to retire? I didn't know you were that close."

Reggie leans slightly over his coffee. In a very low and reserved voice, he replies, "Actually, Jon, I've been obsessing about it for the past three years. There are so many changes going on right now in the printing business I can hardly keep up. In fact, what we are faced with is beginning to scare me. We are moving into a different world than what I have lived and worked in for the past forty years. Right now, our shop is running above average compared to similar operations, but more drastic changes are predicted.

"This summer, I went to the National Printing and Graphics Conference in Vegas. I confess I did roll the dice a few times, tried my luck at the roulette wheel and a few rounds of Blackjack. When I got ahead $100, I figured my good luck was about to run out and quit while I was ahead. I had the same feelings when I attended some of the workshops that discussed succession planning and valuating a business. I came away thinking we have done a pretty good job with Cornelius, but our good luck just may be ready to run out on us."

"Sounds scary to me. Can you tell me more?"

"I became a printer because of my father. It was his business, and he built it into a respectable small-town enterprise during his lifetime. He brought me on board as soon as I could clean the ink rollers and load the paper in his presses. I admired him for his determination and how the people in the community looked up to him as a good businessman and hard worker, honest in his dealings. His formal education didn't match his cohorts in Rotary, of which he was a charter member, but he had their respect. I wanted to grow up to be just like him, which I guess I did. He sent me off to Rochester to learn the latest techniques in printing and graphics and made me his partner within three years after graduating. Together, he and I, we went through some rough times, but we always kept our customers happy, and that paid off.

"We had some scares when the cost of equipment started skyrocketing and ours was getting old and breaking down a lot, but we survived with some fancy business lending with the Avery Bank. That was back in the eighties, and that equipment is still putting out quality print jobs.

"We've had the scare of business being taken away from us because of the Internet, then another because of email, and who knows what's next. I'm glad Father had already died when we were hit with the 2008 recession. We got really low, orders slowed down, and we did some temporary layoffs or shared-work-week hours to keep as many of the employees as we could.

"Twenty percent of our business customers went under and have never been replaced. Fortunately, people still get married and we survived by being the only letterpress printer specializing in wedding invitations in North Georgia. But the high end of that business is now going crazy, with customized hand pieces produced by specialty shops that can charge a fortune for a single invitation and capture enormous profit in all the side paper goods they push on the family of the bride. "Nothing's too good for our Cheryl," and "We only get to marry off our daughter once, so I guess we can afford it."

"We used to be that shop. But now the only orders we get have such a small margin, we can't afford to get involved in the details—we use a mail order system that the bride uses in our office, picking out what she wants. We have them fill out the form on the computer and take responsibility for their mistakes. We just hit the send button. The finished product is delivered to us as though we printed it, and we deliver it to the bride's family with our name on it. But at the end of the day, we have not made more than 10% of the price we charge."

He uses the remaining corner of his waffle to clean the trails of sorghum from his plate and sips his coffee. "That's probably more than you wanted to hear, Jon."

"Actually, that is exactly some of what I wanted to learn about. I'd like to learn more. You mentioned something earlier about the Vegas trip scaring you—some talk or sessions about valuations, I believe, and something about succession planning. Tell me a bit more about that and what it was that seemed alarming to you."

"Are you sure you have the time?"

"I can stay as long as you can, provided we don't need to order lunch here."

"I would expect a minister not to know that much about valuations and succession planning. I have to admit I know less than I should about them for my own business, but in a nutshell, I'll try to explain how they relate to my concerns.

"I'll begin with succession planning. That is what they call getting out of your business after you've had enough of it. Right now, I am feeling pretty done with it and looking for a way out. I would like to retire by the end of next year, in December. Call it quits. I won't be sixty-five by that date, as I'm only sixty now, so I have to be careful about healthcare coverage until I reach Medicare at sixty-five. That will be a challenge with my high blood pressure and borderline diabetes. I believe I could control both of those conditions if I didn't have this business running me ragged.

"So, succession planning is trying to figure out how to exit the business you are in, either through a sale, a closure, or a transfer. If I close the business, I will only get what I can from the equipment and building I own, which wouldn't be enough to keep me and Bonnie comfortable for the remainder of our years. We'd run through our savings and investments in less than ten years, and it looks like if we watch our health and live as long as our parents, we would then be depending solely on Social Security for another twenty years. Not a good way to live out old age, even in Verona. So, the other options are to sell the business, hopefully for a handsome profit, or transfer the ownership of the business to someone else who would keep it going. In the former, the buyer would give us a lump sum payment or spread it out over several years. In the latter, the new operator of the business would continue to share a percentage of the profit until we die or over a set period of years. Am I boring you?"

"Not at all, please continue."

"What was so scary at the conference was the dire warnings that companies like ours will have to make a change anyway in the next few years because of the pressure being put on the industry to compete with the other forms of communication such as the Internet, email, smartphones. Can you believe texting is cutting into our printing business? Anyway, where was I?"

"At the conference, hearing about being forced into some change."

"Oh, yeah, change is coming. The printing industry gurus predict that about a third of the companies in our country, the mom-and-pop shops, will be out of business because they simply can't compete. They will either go bankrupt or just disappear when their owners die. The shops like ours, which are a little bit bigger than what we call a small shop, will face a choice of declining business over five to ten years and loss of value before throwing in the towel or getting picked off by some larger firm. 'Printing vultures' I call them. For pennies on the dollar, they gobble up the regional competition. Right now, so they say, shops our size have a prime opportunity because they are capturing the eye of the big national printing chains that want footholds in strategic markets, like Northern Georgia and the outskirts of Atlanta. Over the next two or three years, the gurus are predicting that good, profitable shops will be paid a premium in the first round of purchases made by the big printing giants. Then the prices will start to fade as the best shops are picked up and the less attractive ones clamor for a buyer at any price. That, Jon, is what is scaring me. And it scares me at the most critical time now that

Mother has passed and an offer is being made for Cornelius Printing."

"I can see how that would be a scary situation. You said something about valuations. How does that fit into the picture?"

"Valuation tries to determine what a business is worth, sort of like an appraisal on a house to test the selling price against what someone is willing to pay for it. Good valuations are usually done by a third-party company, which specializes in that particular type of business sale. After I returned from Vegas, I hired one for my business just to test the waters to see what I was looking at. They were doing a good job of keeping everything very quiet and off the radar until Rex, my bookkeeper, approached me in the presence of Spike to ask about this bill for $25,000 for business valuation services. That opened up Pandora's Box. Spike seemed to take on the air that he had a right to know what this bill was about and what the valuation findings were. I shut him down and told him it was none of his business at this point. Which started a row between us that is still brewing today. If he keeps it up, he could blow a fifteen-million-dollar deal for me. That, Jon, is what is scaring me, and why I came to you. What advice can you give me as my spiritual leader?"

"I'm not sure at the moment. I'll have to think about it. It's new territory to me. I want to learn more to see what insight I might offer. Will you promise to keep me posted? I do want to help."

"Yep, and I'll get the check. It only seems right after what we just discussed. Ethel, we're ready to go here, so tell us the damages."

CHAPTER NINE

I arrive a few minutes early at the reception desk that serves the seven professors in the pastoral care division of Conley School of Theology at Epworth University. While I await Dr. Dan's arrival, I ruminate about developing a systematic approach to funeral ministry. My outline is simple. First, there must be consistency in delivery of care to the bereaved without regard to their status. Second, I can be more efficient in the administration of funeral services if I practice a clearly defined policy and procedures.

I remind myself that Dr. Dan is a proud Virginian, a descendent of the Founding Families of Virginia, a title to remind newcomers that a "Founding Families" bloodline is the equivalent of English royalty. It was his ancestors who attempted to establish a level of dignity that truly represented the Old South. I recall some of what Dr. Dan has shared: he can trace the Dan family name back to the town of Danville, and the Dan River, and hence the textile products that boast the Dan River brand. Dr. Dan might be a professor in Atlanta, but his real roots and loyalty lie in Virginia. This lineage adds to Dr. Dan's air of superiority—his tall stature and erect posture make his six-foot frame seem two inches taller.

Getting back to the point at hand, I will argue two related points: a) Funerals are connections with tradition and dignity, and b) the

DMin program is intended to bring professionalism to the ministry. My proposal to organize the funeral ministry of The Hill and my own ministry will meet those objectives. It is a combination that cannot lose!

Dr. Dan consumes three slices of Veggie Garden at the Pizza Cavern while I nibble on a personal pan pepperoni. Between mouthfuls, he pontificates on how mundane and unchallenging a project on funerals would be to him, to my final review panel, and probably to me.

"Jonathan, surely you have already witnessed that funerals have to be customized for every situation. Of course, you can create some policies and procedures or revise the ones you have at The Hill. But that should take you about two long weekends, one to analyze what you do not have, the other to write up the details and get your staff and elders' approval the next week. It would be a slam dunk for you, and I think you know that. That's why I am not approving it. It's *too* easy!"

He slides another slice of veggie off the platter and in one swift move folds it lengthwise and bites off half of it, then chews three times before swallowing it while I sit stunned at this academic reprimand. Dr. Dan wipes his chin with the paper napkin that is beginning to shred. "Tell me, Jon, what is the toughest area of ministry for you right now? Where are you challenged? And don't tell me it's funerals. I've read your write-up about three of your funerals and you are already a pro compared to some of your peers."

At that moment, I decide to take a huge bite of the pepperoni, so big that it is almost impossible to close my mouth. My intention is to fill my mouth to delay my response, allow myself some moments to think of a reply while I am obviously chewing. Instead, I realize I have just stuffed my mouth beyond its capacity; I can neither chew nor swallow without choking. For a few seconds, I stare at Dr. Dan, feeling my cheeks bulge from the contents of a half-slice of pizza. I have effectively shut myself up, stuffing my mouth to prevent myself from expressing my true anger at the moment toward Dr. Dan's carefully articulated put-down.

I start to gag, eyes watering as my mouth tries to decide what to do with the growing wad. Grabbing my napkin, I cover my mouth to hide its slight opening, enough room to move the pizza dough around a bit. A few small pieces go down the right pipe without me choking. Dr. Dan watches this pause from across the table. I give him a hand signal that I'm okay and just need a moment. It is enough time to distract the focus of his last question.

"Wow, that was too big a bite. I'm so sorry. That's embarrassing. I guess it reveals my nervousness on the subject of my DMin project." I pause and take a sip of Coke to clear my throat and retain a few more seconds to collect my thoughts before responding to Dr. Dan, who just grins and waits.

"I would say there are several areas that really challenge me presently, but not enough to be the focus of a project. There are staffing issues, as always. I just get a music or youth or associate minister in place and begin to see the evidence of their work when search committees start showing up to court them away. I wish there were a five-year rule of no poaching of your fellow staff members. Another challenge is the need for a capital campaign to finish the fundraising for the proposed activities building. The idea was approved in 2006 and the first half million was in the bank before the recession, but it has been dead in the water ever since. We either need to move forward or give the money back. So there's that."

With no appetite, I continue:

"There's also the social issues and stresses for the church, particularly the matter of gender orientation. We are seeing an increase in attendance of visitors who are obviously not the traditional nuclear family. But I'm not sure I want to risk my tenure at this moment by volunteering to tackle that subject. It seems to be a non-issue right now, and I would like to keep it that way."

Enough. Time to toss the ball into the other court.

"What are your thoughts, Dr. Dan?"

"Those are subjects that every other DMin student and every other seminary are addressing, so much so that I am getting bored with the repetition. I'm looking for one of my DMin students to break out into some new territory, and I think you are capable of doing it. I don't know what that is, or how it would go for you."

He sips his iced tea.

"Think for a moment with me. What in your ministry keeps you awake at night? What is the black hole of your ministry, the area where you know the least and probably feel the most vulnerable? Think about that a moment while we order some cheesecake and coffee."

The pizza parlor buzz is fading as frantic students and other diners finish their lunch and head back to classes. Dr. Dan permits a reflective silence to settle across the table to allow me time to think about my vulnerability in the ministry.

With my resistance to dessert weakening, I push my fork into the two-inch thick cheesecake and restart the conversation with a more reflective tone. "I would say that the one area where I feel most lacking in knowledge and least skilled in ministry is in the matter of business and finance. Right now, I am having conversations with a church member who is facing a very serious business crisis. I've never had someone consult me about their business, so I was caught off-guard when he spilled forth his problems to me last week. I've made a stab at circling back and trying to probe a little deeper at what is going on with him. Yesterday, I spent over an hour in a breakfast meeting, listening to him talk about his stress and the agony he's facing over a business decision. He spoke about valuations and business succession planning, all of which made no sense to me. I asked him to explain himself and he did, but the more he explained the more I realized how little I know about business in general."

"I know church business, but not real business. He mentioned something about a fifteen-million-dollar deal and I know my jaw must have dropped. A figure like that seems way beyond my comprehension and my pay grade. So, I guess business—more importantly, business challenges among my church members—is something of a black hole for me. I can't decide about this case this week, whether to dive in or keep my distance and stick to preaching and teaching and weddings and funerals. But I don't see this as a project."

Dr. Dan scrapes away all evidence of the cherry cheesecake on his plate, then looks up at me and grins.

"I think it would make a wonderful project. In fact, it could offer some significant breakthrough in several areas. Remember that the Doctor of Ministry concept began in the 1970s as a way to establish a perspective for ministry as a profession. As you know, it is the highest graduate degree in the field of pastoral ministry. Part of the original idea was to stir up some originality using some practical, local congregational research to push out the boundaries and test new waters in ministry. But over the course of three decades, the projects have begun to fall into a rut, in my opinion. Doing a project to become more aware of business issues as they might impact church life might be noteworthy. I could actually get excited about something like that. Give it some thought, but don't take too long. You need to confirm your project by the end of next month if you want to get your DMin within the allotted time frame."

Driving back to Verona, my mind is spinning with several takeaways from meeting Dr. Dan. How can I explore a ministry connection to business? It sounds so un-spiritual to combine the two. What would my deacons think about a project like this? Where would I go for this research? What would be the thesis and counterpoints?

Pulling into a protected shoulder of Georgia 400, I reach for my cell phone.

"Reggie, this is Jon. I'm glad I caught you. I've been doing some thinking about your situation and wondered if you might have some more time Monday. Don't have time for lunch, but what about coffee mid-afternoon in my office? … Can't do three o'clock? That's okay, 4 p.m. will work for me. See you there. Thanks, Reggie."

CHAPTER TEN

I pour my coffee from the carafe and, half turning with a pouring gesture, ask, "Reggie, I'm glad we could meet this afternoon. Coffee?"

"Sure, might as well. Could use it strong about this hour, but with sugar and two creams. Glad to come over. What's up?"

As I settle down in my chair across from Reggie, I jump-start the discussion. "I've been giving our last conversation a lot of thought. Have you made any progress?"

"Some, mostly on the technical side. I got my accountant involved in the number crunching. Then I met with my financial advisor to see what assets I would need to retire comfortably. I also plan to check with my attorney to see what options I have and how vulnerable I am to legal challenges on this sale opportunity. But I'm still stressing over the family side of the deal. The last thing I want is for it to end up on the front page of the *Verona Times* before it's a done deal. If Spike drags us into court, we'll never get a signed contract."

Reggie clenches his left fist and grips the arm of the wingchair with his right hand. As his face reddens, he continues with a rising, angry voice, "It just pisses me off something fierce to have him threaten to ruin what I have worked for all my life."

He pauses reflectively, releases the arm of the chair and opens his other hand, looking down at his physical reaction. "I just came from Dr. Eberhardt's office this morning, and he is alarmed at my high blood pressure. He wants me to see a cardiologist and run some tests. Not too thrilled about that. Just what I need right now, some health crisis to throw off all this planning."

"I can see how this is really getting to you. Are you getting any sleep?"

"Hell, no! Still staring at the ceiling at 2 a.m., doze off, then staring again at 5 a.m., so I just get up and go into the office and try to work on more details. It is unbelievable all the information the transition company is asking for. Going back ten, twenty years or more. It's crazy! Bonnie is telling me that I'm awfully hard to live with right now. I've told her about the offer from Garnett Press, but I haven't clued her in on Spike's demands. I'm not sure how she's going to take it when she learns about it."

"Do you still have the same concerns about Spike's involvement?"

"Remember what I told you? Spike still wants a piece of the action, some part of the proceeds of the sale. I still find that ridiculous. He has no right. He is not an owner. I'm the only owner now that Mother has passed—God rest her soul."

"Has he said how much he wants?"

"No, he wants to wait and see how much I'm offered before he makes his demands. I told him that what he is doing is jeopardizing the closing of the deal. Here's what I think he'll do. He'll wait until the final offering price is confirmed, then he'll determine how much of that he wants and demand it or else threaten a court-ordered injunction against the sale. If the buyer gets wind of this, or suspects in any way that their offer to purchase is going to be legally challenged, they will just walk away and go to the next seller. They won't fool around with this stuff. There are too many opportunities for them to buy other printing businesses. I've done my research among my colleagues and found several deals where this same company made initial offers, but walked away when it looked like the owners were headed for a spat and some court maneuvering. They just don't have time for that, and I don't blame them. Their idea—and mine, too—is to get to a price that we can shake hands on, then let our attorneys and accountants quietly work out the final details. Then there will be a private meeting where I sign the transfer of title of Cornelius Printing and I walk away with a check."

"So, pardon my ignorance here, and maybe I'm prodding where I don't belong, and you can tell me if I am, but what would be the consequence to you if Spike got whatever he demanded? How would that affect your plans?"

Reggie lets out a deep sigh and slumps further into the chair. "No, you're asking the right question, all right. And you have a right to know the answer if you are going to be of any assistance helping me make a decision.

"Earlier I told you that it's a matter of the numbers, the numbers I need to retire and be able to walk away from this business. The truth is that the offer on the table would be a tight fit for all of that to take place. If Spike somehow siphons off a chunk for himself, it would really change up my retirement plans."

"Well, Reggie, since we are being fully open in our discussion here, I must confess I'm a little lost on this matter. You mentioned something about fifteen million dollars being offered for the business. I have no clue whether that is a good price for your business or not. But when it comes to funding retirement, it would seem to me that that kind of number would be more than ample for a nice retirement nest egg. Am I missing something?"

With a slightly sheepish countenance, Reggie looks down between his feet. After a pause, he responds, "Jon, I can see how that would appear to you. I know what you make here at the church, and some idea of what we have done for your own retirement plan. I admit that it is nothing close to what I have just been discussing about my own condition. What you ask does not anger me. It is sort of embarrassing, I must admit. It probably makes me sound arrogant and ungrateful for what I have. And sometimes, I have to catch myself drifting that way. But without trying to bamboozle you, I have to say it is a bit more complicated than just the sale price of the business and my ability to retire.

"Yes, fifteen million would be a nice nest egg for retirement. But there are a host of issues that have to be considered, including taxes, before I get to fill my retirement account. Yes, I will live comfortably if the business is sold for fifteen million, but that doesn't mean I will have fifteen million in my pocket. According to my financial advisor, Mother's estate attorney, and our accountant, that sale price, after everything is settled, will make it possible for Bonnie and me to have a nice life in retirement, and leave something for our kids and grandkids, maybe travel and have some good times, but it doesn't mean we can go off and live like we are millionaires, even though on the books we will be.

"So, to answer your question, if Spike somehow walks away with a chunk out of this sale, it will seriously change the way Bonnie and I plan to live out my retirement, not to mention what we would like to do for our kids and grandkids. That's the bottom line."

Reggie takes a sip, and I realize I can just wait because more explanation is coming.

"But there is more to it than just the money for the retirement," Reggie continues. "I'm burned out. I have lived and breathed printing since I was a child working next to my dad, cleaning his ink rollers and loading paper in the press. I loved it then, partly because I could work alongside him. I loved the business when I went to Rochester and learned all the latest in graphics and printing. And I found owning and operating Cornelius Printing a source of pride. It gave me a good living, a sense of place in the community. For that, I am extremely grateful. But the work has been exhausting. And the bad times have taken their toll on me physically and on my personal finances.

"Over the years, I have put everything I had into the business. I hocked my house to buy some of the equipment we needed, lived through low salaries for myself—and sometimes lower than the salaries of my help—just to hang on to the business during the tough times, all in hopes that I was investing in my future and my retirement for the moment when I could sell it. I've lived through half a century of printing, from my childhood till now. And I've seen changes, lots of changes, but nothing compared to the pace of changes that are happening now. The fact is, Pastor, I'm tired, done, ready to throw in the towel."

Reggie's pause seems to be in mid-thought. He fidgets, rubbing his left palm with his right fist.

"It came home to me recently when Bill Wrangler, one of my best friends—you know him, he ran the Ace Hardware store here in town. We've been fishing buddies since high school. Well, he keeled over six months ago, dropped dead in his front yard while edging his lawn. My age. All those years we fished and talked about our businesses, and how we were going to retire and take life easy and enjoy our final days with kids and grandkids. And bam! He's gone. He wanted to wait until he was 66 so he could take his Social Security and still work a few days at the store. He had survived the arrival of Home Depot ten miles away, and Lowe's in the other direction. He worked hard all his life, and dreamed of fishing trips to the Ozarks. He had a goal of fishing every reservoir on the TVA between the day he retired and the day he died of old age.

"Got me to thinking how short life really is, how presumptuous we can be about how much time we have left.

"Jon, I'm in okay health for my age, if I can keep this diabetes in check and my blood pressure in line. Both of those will improve dramatically if I can get out from under this business. My parents, both of them, lived until their eighties. My father was very active, traveling, hunting, fishing. I'd like to do what I can to repeat that.

"So, now is the perfect timing for me, and the price is right. Or was right, before Spike stuck his nose where it doesn't belong.

"Is that helpful, Jon?"

We both take a sip, and he looks downward to signal he is finished.

"Reggie, from our conversation, I now understand a great deal more. What you have shared has been very helpful and given me more things to think about. I'm still keeping you in my thoughts and prayers and believe the very best for you. I know you've got to run and I need to check on some folks in the hospital, but this has been very helpful. I've learned a lot. Thank you. Let's get back together soon, say in a few days?"

Rising, Reggie extends and shakes my hand.

"Jon, telling you all this has been helpful to me, as well. Never thought you would have any interest in the nuts and bolts of what is going on in this part of my life. So thanks for listening—and for caring. See you in a few days.

"Oh, one small point. Don't forget to send me Mother's eulogy."

"On it, Reggie, will do."

Before I leave the office, I make a quick phone call.

"Dr. Dan, this is Jonathan Boatwright. I know you are gone for the day, but just wanted to leave you a message to thank you for your frank conversation with me the other day. I've given your advice some serious thought, and I'm ready to present a proposal I think you will like. But I'm going to have to rely on you pretty heavily for some guidance, because what I think is going to be my project will take me into some deep water that right now is way over my head. I'll get my formal proposal to you by Monday of next week.

Talk to you soon."

With my hand on the office door knob, I remember and dart back to my writing table where I pull up on the word processor my last version of Martha Cornelius' eulogy. I run the spell-checker, save it again. After typing a brief line on email to Reggie, I attach the eulogy and hit Send.

Dinner will be waiting.

CHAPTER ELEVEN

Mid-afternoon Friday, I confront a painful truth—two of the hazards of professional ministry are the slushiness of any attempted schedule and the collapse of creative thought. A full week's planning of things to do, people to visit, letters to write, and books to read can be well intentioned on Sunday afternoon and dashed to hell on Monday morning with a week-long crisis that comes from nowhere. And in spite of all the advance planning to outline a preaching theme conformed to the readings of the lectionary, ministry itself must remain loose. Flexibility is essential to sermon preparation.

Four months ago, I had a central idea of the text to guide this week's sermon preparation. Two months ago, I gave Bryan, the music minister, the title and focus text for next Sunday's sermon. Now it is crunch time, only hours remaining to put words onto the monitor. But as is frequently the case, all the well-meaning advance and short-term preparation is now imploding as I doodle around the outline. What was I thinking at the lakeside retreat that would inspire the person in the pew? This sermon is DRT—"dead right there." Any inspiration I might have evaporates while fingers on the keyboard record dry sentences. I'll have to shoehorn this baby into some artificial structure with a half-baked belief.

On a Sunday afternoon, few things are worse than when I actually delivered such a sermon that morning and know it was a dud. The fear of this feeling is beginning to creep into my mind as I attempt several varied sketches for the sermon. The programs have already been printed and folded by Reggie's shop, delivered, neatly stacked on Elizabeth's credenza behind her desk. The publication announces the sermon title: *The Riches of God's Grace,* with a focus on Ephesians 1:3-14. Looking at the program unfolded under my study lamp, I am tortured, trying to tease out what I thought was so important. What was I thinking? What was I smoking? What was I drinking? Where was that Spirit then? Now? Hello?

Squirming in my swivel chair, I edge up to the writing station. In creative epiphanies, ideas and illustrations usually flow easily, so much so that I often must whack away at early drafts, pull in the reins and identify the rabbits I am chasing. In the final manuscript, I only include what is critical, and try to get from the introduction to the conclusion as quickly and clearly as possible. The writing screen digits post 3:07 p.m. I squirm again. The first five pages of this manuscript are wooden. I am pontificating. I imagine for a moment hearing this sermon in the pew and falling asleep at the sound of my own voice. Anger at myself is rising. Foreboding is beginning to take root in the base of my skull, near the muscles tightening at the top of my neck, slowly creeping toward the back of my left ear, followed by a twinkly particle passing in the focal point of my left eye. The warning is unmistakable. A self-induced shutdown is marching in. A migraine. They come whenever I try to reconcile a major incongruity—a battle between what I really believe and what my parishioners think I should believe.

I attempt to restrain a growing temper lest I cause more damage than necessary. I leave the Mac running but flick off the glaring monitor, rise from the writing station and make my way toward my private lavatory. Staring into the mirror, a distraught face stares back. Opening the medicine cabinet, I find the remedy—two Ibuprofen and two Excedrin—then swallow them with tap water.

Moving carefully around the study, I close the window drapes to ward off the glaring daylight, turn off all the lamps and the overhead fluorescents, punch the Do Not Disturb on the phone, lock my door and crawl onto the full-length leather sofa. I have learned the routine battle against this threat the hard way, an experience repeated dozens of times over the years since I started preaching—shut down, don't fight it, back off, trust the Spirit, something will surface. Shut out the light, put the back of my head against the cushioned armrest, my left forearm across my closed eyes, and consciously relax. Check out for the next few minutes. Turn it off. Turn it off.

Sunday morning, I, Reverend Jonathan A. Boatwright, move to the head of the center aisle and begin making eye contact with those sitting in the pew who are silently ready for this pulpit-to-pew monologue to begin. My eyes connect favorite checkpoints—my wife Marsha, the chair of the deacons, little Leslie and her bright green eyes in the third row with her mother, the quiet man in the far back row, the divorcee who still grieves the loss of her husband to a younger version of herself.

Just as my eyes complete a sweep of the congregation, they connect with Reggie's staring back. I am struck by how agonized he looks today, swollen eyes suggesting a hangover. Reggie breaks eye contact, glances down to the center of the pew before him, and then fiddles with a Bible. Seeing Reggie in this distraught condition causes me to flash back to our conversation and his growing angst about Spike. I begin to speak the words I put on paper, memorized and now must deliver because I have nothing else to offer. I force the sermon out of my mouth, feel it go forth with a dryness that makes my tongue stick and words hard to pronounce.

Reggie rises slowly from his seat, steps into the aisle, turns to face the narthex, and with his back to his pastor, his head low and shoulders slumped, walks silently down the red carpet and out the door. I continue dutifully on, my words like small blocks of wood falling from my lips. The brass latch on the big, heavy front door clashes loudly and closes with a *thud*.

"Brother Jon, are you all right?"

Stunned, I whirl to see who is calling, then realize Elizabeth is knocking at the door. A reality check comforts me—I have been dreaming. "Yes, just fine, Elizabeth. Just resting a moment to clear my head," I explain as I crack the door to see her concerned face.

"You were calling out and I thought you needed something. You okay?"

"I must have slipped into a deep sleep and was dreaming. Thanks for calling me back into the world. I'm okay. You need anything?"

"No. I'll leave you alone. Just checking. You've had a few calls, but I told them you were busy and would get back to them."

"Thanks, Elizabeth."

Still a bit swirly from the abrupt rise from the couch, I retreat to the wing-backed chair and try to recall what I just experienced. I turn on the chair-side lamp and as I pull back the drapes, I check my watch—two hours have passed. My headache is gone. But the sermon is still unwritten. Instead of returning to the keyboard, I reach over and pick up my study copy of the *Revised Standard Version*. I review the other readings posted for Sunday to see what inspiration might come from a Plan B.

I am struck right away by the Old Testament reading from Amos, and look again at the description of this ancient prophet, whose name I carry. I always thought of my middle name as a burden. Mom said it was a way to honor her favorite great uncle who lived in Alabama, her family's only real connection to the Confederacy and its dearest sacrifice in the great war. I am always grateful that it was the first name, Jonathan, that held forth as my official school name when I began kindergarten. Only in recent years have I found a re-connection to my nickname, *Jambo*—the family's way of reminding me that my name also honors my mother's family. Now, reading this prophet, my matriarchal connections stand in bold relief, *"The words of Amos, who was among the shepherds of Tekoa…"* For the first time since seminary and Old Testament class, I settle down to see what my Biblical namesake has to offer for Sunday's sermon.

CHAPTER TWELVE

S unday morning, after the reading from Amos, Ephesians, and
the Gospel of Mark, I stand before the congregation on their
level, for real this time. I make my eye-contact ritual, connect
with favorite touch-points, then without notes, begin to speak.

> "There are moments when the best-laid plans of mice and men often
> go awry," so wrote the Scottish poet Robert Burns. Such were the
> moments in the preparation of my sermon today. The original intent
> was to allow the words of the Apostle Paul to guide our thoughts,
> but as the week progressed, Paul ended up getting bumped by a
> predecessor, the Prophet Amos.
>
> I want to spend a few moments telling you about a spokesperson
> for God who did not like to be called a prophet. He preferred to
> be addressed as Amos, a shepherd and dresser of sycamore trees.
> The words of this ancient prophet spoke to me this week on several
> issues that I think are worthy of sharing with you."

I notice during this introduction that my audience response is typical
for the beginning of most of my sermons. I see a scattering of direct
connections with me, the usual who I can expect to have immediate
eye contact. They are ready, open. I also mentally note the usual
majority—fiddling with a purse, re-arranging the books in the pew

rack, sucking on a cough drop, or just checking out for the next few minutes.

I check my demeanor. I am always a mix of calm and nervousness upon entering the preaching moment. I do not relax until the introductory section is passed. But now, I sense an internal trembling. I center on my voice to push on.

> *The prophet Amos and I have something in common. He did not like being called a prophet. And sometimes, I don't like to be called Reverend. Not that the titles of reverend or prophet are dishonorable titles, but in some cases the use of such titles are meant to segregate someone. Instead of honoring the person, the title causes many to discount what that person has to say.*

> *Amos is a good example of that tendency to disregard what someone says because of a perceived title. As he traveled from city to city, he observed how people were treated, taken advantage of—ripped off, actually—all with the blessings of the government of his day. He spoke out against such abuse and his tirades caught the attention of the king. The king, in so many words, told Amos to take his prophetic voice and go back home. He did not belong in the circles of business. "Don't call me a prophet," Amos retorts. "I know what I am talking about, not because you consider me to be a prophet, but because I am a business owner. I know from the inside what is going on and it is not right."*

> *I, too, have experienced such dismissal when it comes to my title as Reverend. In most cases, when someone calls me "Reverend" they are honoring my calling, my role as priest, pastor. And I appreciate that honor. But sometimes, I don't feel very "Reverend." I just want to be me. And there are times when I feel dismissed—my "Reverend-ness" somehow disconnects me from another person. Makes me distant, out of touch. Like Amos, I can be a bit sensitive about titles."*

I can sense the shock that this admission has triggered in some of my listeners. I have more attention than I have previously experienced.

And my heart rate is a bit higher.

> *But more important than our commonality about how we feel about being called a prophet or reverend, is how Amos and I are different.*

> "Amos was a businessman offering two services. He was a dresser of sycamore trees. He was also a shepherd, moving flocks of sheep from field to field and to market. These agricultural ventures took him to business places where he saw firsthand some of the corruption happening in those towns. In the name of God, he spoke out for the consumers and for conducting business fairly and with integrity. He criticized the rulers who condoned abusive business practices. He was equally critical of the religious leaders who turned a blind eye to such behavior. He spoke for God, not as a prophet, but as a business person. Unfortunately, for Amos, he ended up being executed for his outspokenness. This is one point where I hope Amos and I are different.*

I allow the laughter from the congregation to ripple, then settle down. Now that the audience is with me, I prepare for a redirection with a quick pause before continuing.

> *Usually, in religious settings, it is the priest or pastor who receives your confessions. This morning, I want to reverse that process and allow you, if you will, to hear my confession.*

I pause an additional moment for the audience to connect anew, and it does with an unmistakable intensity. I continue.

> *I offer two confessions.*

> "First, throughout my life, I have downplayed my Christian name, the name Amos. I am no longer going to deny my heritage. Rather, I am going to live up to my name.*

> *Second, I realize how very different my ministry is from that of my namesake. While Amos the ancient prophet was immersed more in business than in theology, I, Jonathan Amos Boatwright, have been comfortable discussing the concepts of God and have had*

very little exposure to the real challenges of business life. To you, the business people of Verona and more specifically, all of you who comprise The Hill, who struggle daily in the business world, I offer my sincere apology for not taking seriously the challenges you face. I want to change that.

I realize I do not know what it is like to meet a payroll that provides for the basic needs of employees. I am oblivious to the stresses of multiple levels of regulations, from human resources to OSHA, from meeting demands of the public and demands of shareholders. And I want to change that. The change I seek for myself is not to be more like a business person. Rather, I want a better understanding of how faith is experienced in the tough world of profit margins. So I ask for your help.

I need your acceptance and forgiveness of my shortsightedness and my presumptive perspective in the time we have been together. But I also ask for your help in another matter. I need opportunities to learn more about what you face between Monday mornings and Saturday evenings.

My closing confession is that I do not know where this will go, how it will unfold. This requires me to open myself as a fellow struggler, so that we can learn together. It is my hope that, in what we will learn, we will together grow stronger in faith and as a community of faith.

Where do we begin? I suggest the following first steps:

"I will welcome every opportunity to visit any business, regardless of the nature of that business. If at all possible, I want to see where you spend your days.

I also suggest that we begin having honest discussions, even push back on what I might say from the pulpit, or even read from Scriptures. I suspect that from time to time, you have not always agreed with what I have said in my sermons. You might have thought I was too simplistic, or way out of touch with reality. You might have had the same feelings when we have read passages of Scripture—that there is a big disconnect between what is considered a word from God and where you are in your life or business. I must admit that there are times I feel the same disconnect. My door, my heart, my ears are open.

May this be the beginning of learning, of growing, of caring for each other in new and insightful ways, to the ultimate praise and worship of God.

Amen.

As I turn and step back onto the platform to prepare for the final hymn, Reggie rises from his seat. He begins a single applause and is sporadically joined by others across the congregation—the editor of the *Verona Times,* the pediatrician, the president of the hospital, the proprietor of a truck hauling company, the manager at the bank, the seamstress at the local dry cleaner…more than a third of the congregation stand and applaud not just their pastor, but in praise of God that somehow a bridge is being built between the pulpit, the Word of God, and the tough words of the street.

Stunned, a bit embarrassed by this response, I am also pleased that my words and confession are readily and warmly received. As everyone sings the closing hymn, I begin to ponder what I have just started and if I can live up to what is coming.

CHAPTER THIRTEEN

S unday afternoons at the Boatwright house have a routine, which begins when our family arrives at home in stages after church. Marsha and seven-year-old Amy leave the service as politely as possible after the benediction, followed by Rusty and me thirty minutes later. We guys use the extra time to gather up the sermon manuscript, along with a marked-up copy of the order of worship and last-minute announcements, which we place on my desk. Rusty pins the hand-scribbled notes about people who need appointments or hospital visits onto the note holder next to the phone, in order of importance for Monday morning. While I wash my hands, take off the robe and stole and hang them in the small closet next to the private restroom, Rusty re-orders the pages of the marked-up manuscript and places them along with another clean copy in a folder showing today's date. He then places the folder in my OUT tray for Elizabeth to file. This weekly ritual for my son and me began when he was entering pre-school. He takes great pride in this wrap-up role. He is quick, because the sooner we finish, the more time we have together this afternoon.

By the time we arrive at our home, a cold lunch of sandwiches and chips, a hot soup, or a fresh salad are ready for the family to enjoy as we unwind. The big meal for the day will come later. If the weather is nice, perhaps it will be grilled burgers or bratwurst on the patio, or if inside, a full spread filling the dining table. The first task for Amy and Rusty after cleaning the dishes is to tackle whatever homework is due on Monday morning. The remainder of the afternoon is our personal free time.

My own Sunday afternoon free time begins in my overstuffed recliner in the family room, as I watch a sports event that plays on the big screen, with the Sunday edition of the *Atlanta Journal and Constitution* in my hands. As usual, I am asleep before I complete the *A*-Section, which allows Marsha to gently steal the Lifestyle, the Magazine, and the Travel section before placing a throw over me. This miniature Sabbath lasts about an hour until I wake up and try to recall what I am watching on TV. I return to the *Journal,* casually looking for stories that might add color to upcoming sermons.

I usually skip over the Business section, but not today. I read every story, most of which I do not understand why it is news and why it matters. I am fully aware of how I have never really connected with this medium and it is discomforting. My anxiety rises as I remember my public commitment to connect to the business people of this congregation. I feel threatened as I realize I have very little personal experience from which to launch this new initiative. So I switch my attention and browse through offerings on the big plasma screen: the Golf channel (don't recognize the leaders), NASCAR (one scene of cars approaching and departing looks just like the last scene. Why do they always turn LEFT?), the Braves (where are they playing and whom?), McLaughlin shouting at his guests and viewers, reruns of classic movies on TCM. I hit the Mute button and place the remote control on the armrest, letting the silence sink in while images strobe across the screen.

I am reminded that I am not a very good sports fan. I try to fake it just enough to make light conversation with people whose world is organized sports competition. I have accepted my limitations and do a pretty good job of knowing what to ask. My goal is to direct the conversation in a manner that will require little input from me. All I need to do is nod while the other person rambles on about this star, that manager or the latest statistics.

The same can be said about what I know about business. I do not know enough to ask the right questions to begin a conversation, except "How's your work?" or "How's business?" I let the magnitude of this void sink in as I fold up the Business section. I feel an adrenalin rush that comes when one is threatened. Fearful at what is about to come, I remain in the recliner and try to force myself to relax.

After twenty minutes of pretending, I yield to my anxiety. It is too early to fire up the grill so I go to the garage, start the lawn mower and begin trimming the grass between the back of the garage and the property line that borders the preserve which surrounds our subdivision. Normally I would not carry out such a noisy task on Sunday because the roar of the Briggs and Stratton *might* disturb my neighbors and that would haunt me. "Oh, to hell with it!" I whisper to myself, disgusted at my own self-made dilemmas. I push the mower across the lawn and revel in the difference this machine can make in something so simple as blades of grass.

There is nothing like mowing the grass that is as therapeutic for me. Maybe it's in the relative isolation that I hear myself think above the noise and consider opinions I am reluctant to express openly to others, and sometimes reluctant to say aloud to myself. I have been able to work out some of my most angry moments behind this mower, leaving me wrung-out, but caught up on self-confessions.

Over the course of my adult life in my attempts to seek closeness to God, there have been many mowing meditations—moments with the Divine. I have gone deeper in reflection, experienced more downright epiphanies, than all the times I have attempted the same in kneeling in prayer. It has been on similar lawns in other towns and places that I have processed my commitment to be ordained, or resolved to answer a call to serve particular parishes when all the lists of the pros versus cons had failed to deliver a verdict. So it is, on this particular Sunday afternoon, that I walk behind my mower and entertain ideas of how to connect my ministry with the business community and how that might become my Doctor of Ministry project.

The rest of Sunday afternoon and early evening passes quickly as I finish mowing the side lawn and then proceed to grill a perfect presentation of bratwurst, along with grilled corn on the cob, beside grilled green and red peppers. There is a lightness, a gentleness, that pervades the outdoor patio dinner this evening. I hold my sweetheart's hand as we sit together in the swing, watching our children chase the fireflies in the dusk.

Soon afterwards, I tuck the oldest into bed and kiss Marsha goodnight. I explain that I will be hunkered down in the study for several hours to hammer out the final details of the project proposal due in the morning. I promise to slip into bed by her side when I finish— when I have finally put all the ideas rolling around in my head onto paper.

By three o'clock early Monday morning, I have mapped out a proposal. Over the next six months, I will conduct a three-pronged approach. On a personal level, I will seek out, rather than avoid, the possible connection between business and religion, between faith and profit. I do not propose how I would uncover these connections—that will be the heart of the project.

I will begin with bi-weekly dialogue lunch sessions with the business owners and managers in my congregation. In these sessions, I will encourage two areas of discussion. The first focus will be an invitation to those in attendance to offer feedback and reflection on what has been said in the previous two Sunday sermons, particularly as they relate to the challenges of being a business person. The second area of discussion will be a quick review of the lectionary readings for the next two Sundays. I will encourage each person to offer questions and challenges these readings present to them, with particular insight into their intersection with daily business matters. I will receive these comments without judgment or opinion and reflect upon them in my preparations for worship and sermons for those Sundays.

On a parallel track, I will invite myself to have lunch at least once a week with a business person. I will visit their worksites to learn what I can about the way they spend their days. I want to convey that I am interested, and will go into their world to help connect my ministry and God's word with their world.

I finish the rough draft of my project proposal according to the specifics spelled out in the Doctor of Ministry handbook, but the late hour and associated fatigue will not permit me a properly proofed final edition. I crawl between the sheets and snuggle next to my lover. The last things I see are the green numbers on the nightstand recording 3:40 a.m. I am tired, but not exhausted. Excited, but not panicked. I fall quickly asleep, but I am very much alive!

❧

By ten o'clock Monday morning, I have proofed my proposal, completed all the cover pages, checked off the list of items that Epworth requires and submitted my creation to Dr. Dan by email. By eleven o'clock, Dr. Dan is on line one, ready to discuss the idea at hand.

"Nice work, Jon. I see you took me seriously. I think you are going to stretch both of us with this project. I hope you have time to walk through each part. Let's start with the results you hope to achieve and move on to your research methodology."

For the next hour, Dr. Dan and I banter back and forth about the challenges ahead of us, and how to deal with them. The biggest initial hurdle is our mutual lack of business acumen. We admit our exposure to the nuts and bolts of real business is limited to our part-time jobs while in seminary. I worked in sales on the floor of Davidson's Department Store, and spent a few summers in shipping and receiving. I know housewares, the wholesale prices and the markups, but don't understand the rationale behind those numbers. Dr. Dan was a day laborer on construction crews, and his observations of business were limited to how much time it took to dig a ditch for a footer and the ratio of mortar mix, sand and water.

Granted, over the years we both had experienced in church ministry the tough process of balancing operating budgets, but any consideration of a profit margin had been taboo. Where we are headed will also include the tough world of taxes on every level of operation—property, employment, sales, inventory, and profit. Profit is a topic neither of us is familiar with because of our unique tax exempt status. We both have expertise in theology and church history, communication and pastoral care through years of either experience or teaching. Where will we turn to pick up the essentials of business without committing to another degree on the subject?

We agree on timelines for the completion of specific phases of the project. During the next week, we will each think about what we know, what we do not know, and where we might go to find it.

On the following Monday morning, the discussion continues. I want to pursue a deeper study of the role of business and economics in Scripture. I suggest beginning with the prophet Amos and then include other prophets and the historical narrative of the Hebrews around the subject of enterprise before jumping into the Gospels, the Epistles and the history of the Church. I can tell I have whetted Dr. Dan's academic curiosity, but the research must respect reasonable boundaries.

It is the typical approach for academia—the professor with the terminal degree encourages her graduate students to wade through the material and then surface with the most pertinent data necessary to prove or challenge a theory. The professor uses these gleanings for classroom lectures and academic publications, with a tip of the pen to the assistants. The professor satisfies her thirst for pieces of information and assimilation of large pools of data. The rising graduates learn to move quickly through material and determine the difference between what is useful for the project and what is good trivia, but probably irrelevant in producing results. This allows both the professor and the assistants to impress those who know less but always wanted to know more.

There is one information arena that is out of reach for both Dr. Dan and myself—the daily experiences of the business person. I cannot dismiss my obligation as the pastor of a prominent community church and become an actual business owner. But what I can do is begin listening, being truly present with the business owners and managers that make up my community and congregation. To be present demands more than showing up at the sales counter or business office lobby and looking around. It cannot be captured in a "fellowship" meal around sandwiches at the coffee shop. To be present will require listening for the pain, the joy, the frustration, the challenges and the opportunities that are ever present in commercial enterprises.

To that end, Dr. Dan and I refine the project. I will commit one half-day a week to be present with a member of my flock in their environment. Ideally, I hope to show up after the start of their workday, spend a few hours taking a tour of the business and discuss what they produce or what services they deliver. We might wrap up our time together with a lunch.

Dr. Dan and I have at last outlined the project's research methodology—it's the hardest part, he assures me. For the next three months, I will try to get a handle on the issues facing the local business people of my community. Hopefully, I will find a way to bring the two worlds together in a way that mutually strengthens our spiritual journeys.

CHAPTER FOURTEEN

L ast week, I ordered two commentaries on Amos the Prophet. They arrived Saturday and I quickly absorbed the scholarly information then put the volumes aside to reflect on this ancient character. I recall some wisdom from one of my professors of Old Testament, who explained that there were hundreds if not thousands of so-called prophets in every period, and therefore a myriad of views about the present and predictions about the future. It was easy to be a prophet. All you had to do was read the equivalent of the current newspaper and express your opinion—and be willing to die for that opinion. Digging down into the details about Amos, I was reminded that he was a bit of a maverick in his day. And, typically, it got him killed.

"Do I dare risk getting into the business world?" I ask myself. *"I am protected by both religious liberty and a constitutional due process of law. But I find myself a bit uneasy. I would like for this Amos to live a long, healthy, happy life."*

Near daybreak Tuesday morning, I turn my Ford Five Hundred into the gravel entrance on Industrial Boulevard and scan the field of heavy earth-moving equipment to find an office building or familiar face. Fifty yards ahead, I spot Ed "Max" Maximillian, the owner of ReMaxEx Construction Company, Inc. Max called me Sunday afternoon to express how my words had resonated with him. He wanted to be the first to take me up on my offer to learn more about a business in the community and the people in it. "Show up at 7 a.m. at my place and I'll get you started. Wear some work clothes because we are going to tour some rough sites and do a lot of walking."

I had not pressed the issue that my work clothes consist of a coat and tie, but I took the cue to "dress down." I shopped at The Tractor Supply over in Canton and purchased a pair of tan work boots and two pairs of thick socks. I didn't bother to scuff them up to pretend that I was a field worker, but I did wear an old pair of worn Levi's and a short-sleeve plaid shirt. Not knowing what to expect, I am both excited and anxious about this venture and concentrate on being open to whatever comes my way. I park the car in line with six pickups and make my way to the cluster of a dozen men standing around the front entrance of the office.

Max extends his hand. "Morning, Jon, glad you're here. This is Bo, Chuck, Bill, Toad, Miller and Bud. Guys, this is my pastor and I've invited him to tour our operations with me today. You'll see him riding around with me."

They all nod toward me and each sticks his hand out. I respond with a firm handshake, my white hand completely engulfed in their dark, tanned grips.

"We'll see you guys along the way. Be safe, be careful, and be accurate. No sloppy work. No repeats. Watch out for the guys on the ground. And don't tailgate."

They each whirl away toward their assigned orange pickup. Max places his hand on my shoulder and motions for us to enter the office building. We walk across an entrance lobby of green linoleum tile marked with attempts to sweep up the bulk of the dust from muddy shoes. Hard, durable steel chairs with deep green seat pads and backs line the walls of the room. The florescent ceiling fixtures buzz, one blinking, casting an off-yellow light. At the end of the room sits a very large woman wearing a hands-free headset slightly cocked, talking loudly to the caller as if he or she is standing across from her cluttered dusty desk. She is obviously in damage control mode. Max waves at her as he leads me back to his office at the end of the twenty-foot corridor. All along the wall of the hallway are framed aerial photographs of land with sprawling lines of roads and new rooftops. Lettering in one corner identifies the subdivision and the date of the photo.

Upon entering Max's private office, I notice an eight-foot drawing board propped against the wall, covered in layers of blueprints with details of culverts and bridges. To the side of Max's cluttered desk are two large leather chairs at a ninety-degree angle to each other, a collapsible serving stand between them. Max motions for me to take one of the seats while he places his clipboard among the pile of other documents, stacked next to the phone with six blinking red lights.

Before I have a chance to think about what I might say, the woman previously at the front desk appears at the entrance to the office. In one swift move, she places a cup of coffee in Max's hand and a fistful of pink slips of paper on top of his clipboard. Turning to me, she asks gruffly, but with a slight smile, "How do like your coffee, Rev?"

"Black is fine," I respond.

By the time Max sorts the pink slips, tossing half of them into the trash basket, the woman returns with a stained cup filled with steaming coffee and places it on the table between the two chairs. She then stands with her arms crossed at the front of Max's desk, waiting for his attention.

"Hilda, this is my pastor, Jonathan Boatwright, who I told you about yesterday. Jonathan, this is Hilda Weber. She runs the place and keeps me and all my guys in our place, but I told her to go easy on you this first day. She can be a bitch, but she is my darling. Keeps me out of trouble—most of the time."

"How do you do, Father," Hilda offers with a slight German accent. "Nice to meet you. Max said to treat you like the rest of them, so pardon me if I slip up and let out a few words now and then that you're not used to hearing. You'll just have to forgive me if I ever show up to confession."

She smiles, her wide grin revealing a chipped bicuspid, and extends her hand, her grip more vice-like than with the crew outside. She whirls around and exits the room.

"Hilda." Max exhales with a slight air of embarrassment. "Hard to be around her at times, impossible to survive when she's not here."

"So, Brother Jon," Max continues as he settles into his side chair askew to mine. "You showed up, and I'm glad you did. I'm not sure what you want to do on this visit, but I really like what you said and thought I'd give you a shot."

"Thanks, Max. I really appreciate the invitation. I'm not sure what I'm looking for at this point. I just realize I know very little about the places and conditions where most of the people I know spend most of their waking hours. I don't want to interfere with your business. But I do want to learn about the biggest delights and the biggest concerns that you live with in your business—what makes you go each day, what disturbs you, what keeps you awake at night, and what makes it all worth the effort."

I take a few sips and continue, "So, honestly, I'm just exploring, listening. What would you like to tell me about your business, your workday? What do you think I need to know?"

"Jon… Can I call you Jon?"

"Please!"

"Jon, this is all new territory for me, as well. I've never had this request before. Never seen any interest at all from your types in what I really deal with every day. So I don't have a clue either on where to begin." He takes a sip from his cup then continues, "So here we are, two novices at this project. Kind of makes us equal, wouldn't you say?"

"Indeed. Right away, I'd like to know how you came to this type of business."

"It's a long story. I'm glad you asked, and I'm glad to share it. But give me just a few minutes to return a couple of critical calls and I'll fill you in as we drive out to the worksite."

During the next few minutes, I listen to Max carry on technical conversations with the people on the other end of the calls—details about measurements, timelines, and the price of repair on the hydraulics for the front-end loader that needs to be back online the next day or the schedule will fall behind. When the last critical call ends, we exit Max's office and make our way down the hall toward the front. Max stops at each office door, ushers me in ahead of him, and introduces me to each person, explaining their responsibilities. I meet Amber, the Vice President of Pre-development and Proposals. She is responsible for the company's purchase of large acreages and works through the zoning and mapping stages for local county approval.

In the next office, he introduces me to the Project Director, Bill Monroe, responsible for scheduling and day-to-day operations to see each project through from the date of its approval by the county until it is turned back to the county as a public right of way.

At the third office, Max introduces the Vice President and Chief Financial Officer, Mildred Connifer, who keeps all the records straight and also oversees the projects from their initial bidding to the collection of the final payments along with payments to all the sub-contractors and suppliers. She also serves as the Human Resources Officer, which takes care of the payroll, hiring, firing, and benefits for the ninety employees.

As we complete the tour of the hall offices, Max bids farewell to Hilda with a wave so as not to disturb her conversation on the headset. Immediately outside the entrance, Max motions me to take a left.

"Before we go to the site, let me take you out to the garage."

We walk about fifty yards across a gravel pathway and enter a large metal barn where several pieces of heavy equipment are in various stages of disassembly. A forklift raises a tire taller than me onto an axle that is even with my shoulder. Two assistants guide the alignment by hand. I notice that there are at least a dozen employees in overalls working in this huge shelter and all of them wear hearing protection. Max hands a grimy set to me and motions to put them on. Surprisingly, I am amazed at how these devices dull the roar of the engines and enhance the sound of the human voice, which allows Max to introduce Charles, the shop foreman in charge of maintaining all of the machines. There is not much conversation to exchange beyond introductions, but Max conveys that this spot is critical to their overall operations and brags about Charles' integral role.

"He runs the most critical department of our entire operation," Max shouts. "Every hour that our equipment is down is costing us money and profit. He keeps us running at top potential. Thanks, Charles. Talk to you later!"

As we make our exit, we hang the ear gear on pegs fixed to the framing of the huge sliding doors.

At Max's direction, I climb into a cinnamon red Cadillac Escalade with no markings except for the tag *RMAXEX1* and buckle into the passenger seat. The sealed air-conditioned cabin is a relief from the Georgia heat as we pull out of the ReMaxEx headquarters lot toward a destination unknown to me. Though it is a spacious, high-end luxury SUV, most of the space is filled with a laptop computer with the screen open and tilted toward the driver. Immediately overhead is a custom-installed two-way radio system with various colored lights emitting voices mixed with waves of static. The back seat has various books and binders stacked at precarious angles, and along the floorboard are rolled up blueprints.

"Jon, we're going to visit three work sites this morning. The first one will be the site of a new hospital project on the north side of town. We are preparing the ground for a four-story, 100-bed North Georgia annex of the CINCA Health System. Then we're going to see the progress on a 250-home development about five miles beyond that. And finally, we will check out the wetland project we are building.

"You asked earlier how I got into this business. I guess you could say I got started in college. My dad was a mortician who owned a large funeral home and cemetery in Dothan, Alabama. He wanted me to follow in his footsteps and eventually take over the family business, and offered me a full ride at the mortician school in Atlanta. But I realized I would never fit the mold of a mortician and my dad came to the same conclusion when he saw my mortuary school grades. So he sent me instead to Auburn to study business. Loved Auburn, still do.

"While I was at Auburn, I worked part-time for my uncle Ted, on my Momma's side, in the afternoons and on weekends, and full-time each summer. He owned a scrap metal yard halfway between Auburn and Columbus. I started out sorting metals and helping customers weigh their scrap. Before long, Uncle Ted let me get some experience on the front-end loader, then the crane, and finally driving the big dump trucks and tractor-trailers. By the time I finished with my business degree, I knew how to operate and repair every piece of equipment he owned. While I was tired of being around the scrap yard all day, I loved the equipment. My roommate's father owned a small excavation company in East Georgia near Augusta and was ready to hand it off to his son. So we worked out a deal for the two of us to take over his business. We renamed that business Buddy Max Excavation, using our first names, and the business took off. So, that is how I got started."

"So, how did you end up in North Georgia with ReMaxEx?"

"Our business went under in the 2001 recession and I moved up here, picked up another small business and started over. We bought cheap, paid cash, laid low, waiting for the turnaround. When it came, we were ready with more equipment and a pool of skilled workers that allowed us an edge up on the competition. We haven't stopped growing since."

"You say 'we.' Is there more than you in the business?"

"Yes, my silent partner is my father-in-law. He made a small fortune in the stock-trading business back in the day and never wanted to go back. He is in his late seventies now, and he trusted me with this business. Here we are at our first site for today."

Through a light-orange dust cloud I see heavy equipment moving in patterns. Max parks the Escalade near the construction trailer and we step out onto the packed red clay.

"Here, put this on. OSHA requirements," as Max tosses me a white safety helmet. "And this, too. It's a safety vest so I can tell where you are. Just adjust the straps to fit it over your shoulders and around your waist. That's good."

As I connect the straps across my chest I'm thinking how ridiculous it would have been for me to be here in a coat and tie. Glad I interpreted "work clothes" correctly.

"Hello, Rick." Max shouts. "Looks like everything is off to a good clip this morning. The culverts for the back run-off into the retention pond were re-ordered for the right size and should be here by Friday. Rick, this is Jon Boatwright, my pastor. He's riding shotgun with me today to see what it is I do with my time. Jon, this is Rick Sanchez, he is the foreman on this site."

We shake hands and Max leads the way into the construction trailer.

The closing door shuts out the roar of diesel engines and back-up beeping. After about fifteen minutes of discussion on matters foreign to me, something about pitch, thousands of yards of fill, rip-rap, and the weather, we all shake hands and Max thanks Rick for the update. We head back out the front door and climb back into the SUV. Max takes a tour of the site, pointing out to me what each piece of equipment is doing, how it is doing it, and why. Then, bouncing across the pocketed field and dodging the mud puddles as best as he can, he heads northward on the highway. The computer is beeping. He taps the screen with his index finger, causing the sound of a dial tone, then an answer by a familiar voice.

"Hilda, what's up?"

"The damn son of a bitch from Georgia Power is acting like a true asshole, and I had to threaten to give him a bigger one before he would get his shit together in order to get that goddamn power re-connected to the trailer at the wet site.… Oh, shit. The preacher's sitting right there, isn't he?"

"Yep," clips Max, immediately followed by the dial tone at Hilda's initiation.

"She's a little rough around the edges, Reverend. But she means well. And she gets the job done. None better at it than her. I apologize."

"Well, it is what it is, Max. No apology needed. If I'm going to expose myself to the kitchen, so to speak, I can't be offended by the heat. Where are we off to next?"

"We're headed for the Walton Project about five miles north. It's a high-end luxury estate subdivision. We're putting in the roads and infrastructure, including utilities, the basic clearing for a golf course, and a hundred-acre lake."

During the ride, Max is continuously communicating by one of the two cell phones he carries, the two-way radio, the laptop computer at his right elbow, or sometimes a combination of all four. His multitasking at 70 mph gives me the shivers. I silently remember the lyrics of several hymns. I'm thinking *Just a closer walk with thee* would do fine right now.

Max handles the report of a no-show sub-contractor. The absence of a sub-foreman. A tractor trailer hauling logs to the mill has broken down on Georgia 500 with a busted hydraulic line. He turns off the highway onto a secondary road for a quarter mile then again to the right on an unpaved roadbed covered in potato-size gravel for about a half mile. Coming into a clearing, I see fifty-year-old oaks and loblolly pines toppled like weeds by bulldozers. Two cranes operate on the other side. One uses a massive saw blade to shear the huge trunks into twenty-foot lengths. The other loads the broccoli-like tops into the top of a roaring grinding machine that spits out a spray of green and white chunks onto a pile thirty feet tall. Max pulls up opposite a gold and orange Chevy Suburban, so he can talk across to the driver's window to the bearded man sitting behind the wheel.

"What's up, Joe?" he shouts above the roar of the saw and grinder. Joe nods a thumbs-up and exchanges a half-dozen rounds of shouts indicating the previous problem is solved and everything is moving according to plans. Max finishes the conversation by closing his window, then turns immediately to the laptop to enter some of the information and details he has just received from Joe. We make a wide, bumpy U-turn and retrace our entrance, driving slowly at first to observe carefully every piece of equipment in operation. I take it all in without comment, careful not to disrupt Max's agenda.

Max restarts the conversation.

"That project is one of the biggest we have taken on in the past two years. Nice to see signs that the economy is turning around. The houses that are going in here are expected to list for no less than two million on ten-acre lots. The major realtor for this project is using a helicopter to fly in prospective buyers from as far away as Charlotte. They expect to sell out before the first home construction begins. It's beyond my pay grade, but it sure is fun to work on."

Max reaches into a side door pocket and pulls out a pouch of Red-Man chewing tobacco and gestures a first access to me. I wave off the invitation but am pleased to be included. He pinches a wad with two fingers and a thumb and forces it into his left cheek. As soon as the wad is settled in his mouth, he continues. "Jon, are you getting what you are looking for?"

"Indeed, Max, and I thank you for this experience. It is an eye-opener. Never realized all that goes on in the preliminary development of land. Absolutely amazing."

"It's really just a bunch of grown boys playing around in the dirt, and getting paid quite nicely for it. I love my work. Love being out in the fields, running between the projects, rain or shine, snow or scorching hot.

"I know I've thrown a lot at you, these past few hours but I want you to feel free to ask any questions you would like. What would you really like to know?"

"Thanks, Max."

Immediately, Max responds to an incoming call from Hilda, this time with carefully guarded words that makes the information seem less important. As the conversation concludes, I pick up on the invitation for questions.

"Max, I'd be curious as to what keeps you awake at night. When it comes to this business, what worries you the most?"

"I'd say what keep me awake at night are three things—Safety. Safety. And Safety. My daily goal is that everyone goes home every working day in as good a shape as the hour they arrived on the job."

"Have you had some issues in the past?"

"Yes, two of them. They still haunt me from time to time."

Max pauses, and I wait. We ride another mile in silence. Then Max re-starts the conversation.

CHAPTER FIFTEEN

"Several years ago, in my first company, we were working on a major operation over in East Georgia, a power plant. One of our ground crew was killed, backed over by a grader and crushed to death. She left behind two young children and a husband. The guy operating the grader went crazy for a while and had to be hospitalized."

"What happened?"

"She was part of the ground crew that monitors the laying and leveling of fill dirt, giving the operator signals with flags as to how much more is needed and where. The operator thought she was off to the right and backed right over her. They were both tested for drugs and luckily they each turned up negative. It sent a shockwave through our entire company. And then, as you might expect, the family sued us and the operator was charged with negligent homicide. He was cleared, but the suit went on, with some big-time accident attorneys making us look like villains. It was tough to take. It went to trial by jury and, of course, her family won. The claim was three million. However, we were found to be only fifty-percent liable. The insurance paid out a million four and we had to come up with our deductible of a hundred thousand."

"Why were you only liable for half the claim?"

"To put it kindly, the autopsy revealed the employee was found to be a bit hung over from a party the night before. It was also a cold morning. She was wrapped up in a hooded parka and her vision was partly blocked. Also, when they found her, she was wearing the ear protectors, but she had ear buds running into them and was listening to something on her iPod. She was held to be partly responsible for her own death. Still didn't make it any easier.

"Then OSHA came down on us hard. They charged us with failures in our safety policies and inadequate safety training and supervision, fined us $250,000, which ended up taking all the profit out of that project. But we survived that."

Another quarter mile passes in silence before I attempt to carry the conversation forward.

"You said there were two major safety incidents."

"Yes, the second happened six months following the conclusion of the trial for the first one. One of our sub-contractors had left our site and was pulling a utility trailer carrying a small Ditch Witch trenching machine. The driver went over a bumpy bridge and the bump popped the trailer from the hitch, causing the trailer to careen off into the oncoming traffic. Sliced through a Pinto carrying four workers, two of them ours—a husband and wife. The husband was killed instantly and the wife, who was eight months pregnant, was busted all to pieces. By some miracle, she and the baby survived—born while she was still in a coma. Another passenger was seriously injured and the Pinto driver didn't survive.

"Turns out the driver of the truck pulling the trailer had failed to secure the trailer to the ball hitch, and also failed to connect the safety chains between the truck and the trailer. In addition, the sub-contractor had allowed his vehicle and liability insurance to expire, so the power company made us the secondary liability to a ten-million claim from all the families involved.

We saw no need to go to a jury trial on that one, but the judge awarded the plaintiffs fifteen million. We were only covered up to a max of ten. The settlement that our insurance company did pay covered the first ten million, but left us holding the bag for the remaining five. No insurance company would carry us from that point forward. That's the part of the bankruptcy story I didn't reveal earlier. It wasn't a matter of bad business decisions. It was simply one of those terrible accidents that can not only take away lives and cause serious injury to people who may or may not be your employees, but it can make a lifetime of work and success come crashing down around you."

"How did you get through all of that? I can't imagine living through something like that."

"Well, it did push me off the deep end."

Max pauses his conversation and fiddles with the A/C levers.

"I started coping—or not coping, as you might say—by drowning my sorrow and failure in booze, then moved on to coke. Lost my marriage, access to my kids, before I hit bottom and went into rehab. Got my stuff together eventually, and started all over again. Met Amelia, thank God, and we started another life together ten years ago. With the help of her father providing the financial underwriting, we started ReMaxEx right at the bottom of the recession. It turned out to be perfect timing, and here we are today."

"That's an amazing journey. Based on all that, you say it is safety that might be the one thing that keeps you awake at night. How are you doing with that area now?"

"When I started ReMaxEx, once I had a crew, my next priority was to hire a safety officer. My first one was Tom. He's still with me and you'll meet him on the next site. I have three safety officers now, one on site for each project. Their job is to monitor everything we do, be aware of every possible threat or weakness we might have with regards to safety and address it immediately, even if it means shutting down operations. They are actually safety engineers, trained to be aware of OSHA and any other regulations. They provide on-site as well as classroom training for every employee. We have monthly training sessions, usually on days when it is too wet to work in the fields. We drive home the matter of safety, not just 'be safe out there' but 'Here is how you, Ricky, need to practice safety for yourself and the crew around you.'"

"How is that working for you?"

"So far, and knock on wood, ReMaxEx has yet to have an OSHA violation, and we have one of the lowest claim rates for workers compensation in the state for our industry. Our ability to win the bid on these three projects you're seeing today is not because of price but because of our attention to safety. The companies that choose us like the way we do business in that area. The last thing they want is bad PR or a claim coming against them for some death or injury that's the result of negligence of one of their contractors."

Max steers the Escalade down a narrow muddy lane through the woods before stopping at a site obviously under construction, but unlike anything I have seen on the two earlier stops. Max points out the differences. Trees with big root balls covered in wet canvas and tarps stand like a line of soldiers, tags banded to their trunks. Thirty-foot mounds of dark soil are spaced out around the cleared acreage.

"This is going to be what we call a man-made wetland. Remember the first site, the hospital expansion? Part of the five-year delay in getting that project started was regarding the land the hospital bought eight years ago, which they thought was just plain farm land, grazing fields for cattle. But the environmental boys produced evidence that the 100-acre area had been a wetland before the 1940s. In the 1950s, it had been stripped of its timber, drained of its swampy conditions, and made into a pasture first for pigs and then cows.

"The EPA said no way on the project. If any changes were to be made to that acreage, it had to be restored to its original wetland conditions. The hospital pushed back with all the political leverage they could muster and eventually negotiated a deal. The EPA would allow the hospital to move forward with its intended construction, if the hospital went out somewhere in the county, no more than five miles away, and constructed a 150-acre wetland for environmental compensation. So that's what we have here. We're actually building a swamp, complete with mud, cypress and water oaks. We are redirecting the water flow so it collects here and starts a habitat for waterfowl. Go figure!"

Accompanied by a delightful chuckle from Max, we climb out of the SUV and make our way to a ten-foot by ten-foot construction shack with a hand-painted sign on cypress wood stating "Little Okefenokee Headquarters." Coming toward us is a thin man in his late thirties. He swings from side to side in his gait, which indicates use of prosthetic legs from the knees down. He extends a left hand, which Max matches in a handshake. I quickly note that the man's right hand holding the clipboard is also prosthetic, so I extend my left following Max's lead.

"Tom, this is Jon. He is my pastor and is riding shotgun with me today. Jon, this is Tom Halverson. He is the safety officer for this project. He is helping us with those issues we were just talking about. And thanks to Tom's oversight, we have no loss of days due to injury on this site. We're going to keep that record growing, right, Tom?"

"Yes, sir. Everything within our power. Everybody goes home, every day!"

"We're not going to stay long. Just touching base with you. Any issues today?"

"Everything is running according to schedule. Seems like everybody is finally getting the message that safety is a priority at ReMaxEx."

"Then we're off back to the office. See you at the managers' meeting Thursday afternoon. Say hello to Mary and the kids."

Max turns to lead me back to the SUV. As we begin our return route to the office, Max adds, "Tom is a life-saver, for real. He lost his legs and the arm in combat in the Iraqi war, took some damage on his own as an officer to save some of his troops. Now he is saving lives on jobs like this.

"You know, I could stand before the guys daily and preach safety and they just blow me off. They think they've heard it all before and I'm just going through the motions to satisfy OSHA or some other regulation. But when Tom stands before them, he gets their attention. What he says, sticks. He doesn't take any bull when it comes to setting an operator straight on a safety procedure. He watches the operations like a hawk, and he'll listen to the operators, but he'll also learn everything he can. His background in the Army was with the heavy combat engineers, and he damn well knows what he's talking about. And they listen. And it pays off."

While Max reconnects with the computer messages and returns phone calls as we head back to the office, I ponder the wide scope of what I have just witnessed in the few hours of riding shotgun with Max Maximillian. Back at the company headquarters, I wrap up the visit with gratitude:

"Max, this morning has been an eye-opener. What I never realized was all the burden you carry in running your business. I worry about using the right words at the right time. But you have the risk of lives in your hands. Wow! What an education you have given me. Thank you."

"Pastor Jon, it has been my honor or to show you around. And I'll probably pay more attention to the words you use."

The parting handshake seems, at least to me, to have more warmth and connection than the earlier greeting.

As I make my way back home to change into *my* work clothes, what strikes me is how shielded I am as a pastor. I'm not responsible for the safety of people working in the midst of equipment that can snuff out lives. I don't need to bid for jobs that risk my home and assets in order to work and make a living. I worry about people who must be admitted to hospitals but give no thought to how they are built nor how much it costs. If I make a mistake in a sermon, or calling someone by the wrong name, some people might get upset or even angry and disappointed in me. But I'm not responsible for decisions that cost people their jobs and perhaps their lives. Yet I am psyched by what I have learned about another world of work and about myself. And I'm eager to learn more.

CHAPTER SIXTEEN

It is Tuesday and I have only three hours to honor my double deadline. First priority—a sermon title for Sunday week with focus Scripture reading confirmed for Bryan. Second priority—a detailed outline and first sketch of the sermon to be preached in five days. To avoid the weekend migraines, I must put aside for the moment all that I have taken in during my ride-a-round with Max. I buckle down to the hard work of sermon preparation. Looking over my scheduled sermon plans I have carefully mapped out to match the lectionary readings, I realize that now is not the time to restructure those plans.

My time with Max re-enters my thoughts. I need to learn more about other businesses in my congregation before I start exploring the application of faith and business. It will be several months before I feel comfortable speaking realistically about the integration of what might be two opposing disciplines.

It is three o'clock and I have met both deadlines. Relieved, I push my chair back from the writing desk and whirl around to face the business of running a church and the attendant stack of call-back pink slips Elizabeth brought to me while I was buried in the previous deadline ruminations. At the top of the stack of six slips is a message from Reggie requesting lunch tomorrow. In a quick call, we confirm the details.

As I meet Reggie, I expect a dramatic update, but soon realize he just needs to be in touch as he tries to resolve the sale offer.

"Do you have any insights?" he asks quietly.

"You've been in the forefront of my thoughts and prayers. Can't say that I have any specific advice. I'd like to talk to Spike and see what he is thinking. Maybe I can get a better handle on being able to advise you. Would you mind?"

"Jon, I would welcome it, but I'm not so sure how Spike would take it. The Hill is not exactly his favorite house of worship. He thinks we are all going to Hell because of our liberal ways, that we are a bunch of stuffed shirts when it comes to religion. So, I'm not sure you will get a warm response."

"Thanks for the caution," I reply. "In order to begin that conversation, I need some freedom to speak frankly about what I have learned, mostly from you, about the situation. Can you give me that freedom?" I pause for a moment to let that request register, then continue. "Sounds like Spike, from what I've seen and what you've said, is a pretty straight-up, no-nonsense kind of guy who cuts through the fancy talk and just comes right out and says what's on his mind."

"Oh, you're being kind there, Jon. You have no idea!" Reggie rolls his eyes for emphasis. "But yes, you can say that we have talked. I'd like for you to keep the specifics out of the conversation, though. You know, the offer amount for the business, some of my strategy. But yes, if you can steer clear of sharing that information, go ahead. I'm eager to hear what he might tell you."

"Ah, and there's the catch. I might not be able to tell you all that he tells me, without his permission. It works both ways. I need to go forward in these conversations with as much fairness as I can.

So, I can't promise you that I am going to run back to you and tell you everything that Spike says to me. And vice versa. But having conversations with both of you might help me understand more of the challenges you both are facing."

"What have I got to lose?" He nods with resigned consent and a grin.

Driving back to the office, I place a call on my cell.

"Spike, this is Jonathan Boatwright. Thank you for taking my call. I know you are busy at work and I only want to take a minute. I was wondering if you would be willing to meet me for breakfast or lunch one day this week. I can explain the reason for my request at that time. It would be very helpful to me…

"Okay, seven a.m. tomorrow at Denny's. I'll see you there. Thanks, Spike."

After we greet and claim a booth in the back during the breakfast rush hour, I begin the conversation with the typical icebreaker around the weather—how hot it is this summer. And we chat about vacations already experienced or planned before the school year starts again. After Spike orders a full breakfast platter and I request a Texas omelet, we both sip our coffee and I focus on the purpose of our meeting.

"Spike, thank you for meeting with me this morning. You're probably wondering what this is all about."

Spike yields a toothy grin. "I guess it has something to do with Reggie's business deal that's coming up. Are you going to try to get me to see it his way?"

"Actually, you are right on half of that. Yes, part of my request to meet is about your brother's business deal. But, no, I have no intention of trying to get you to see it his way. As you might imagine, he has shared with me quite a bit about the offer that is on the table and also some of his concerns about your connections with the proposed transaction. I have asked him for permission to speak with you. What I suspect is that there is another side to the story I'm hearing. I'd like to hear your side."

"What has my big brother told you?" he asks with a touch of smirk.

"Without revealing anything considered confidential, he has been offered an opportunity to sell the business. You have gotten wind of this offer to some extent. And you want a say and perhaps a share in the sale, if that sale occurs."

"Yes, that's the quick and dirty of it. Why is that such an unusual request?" Spike cocks his head slightly and juts his chin. "It was our father's business. The business took care of our mother until she recently passed, and now it is up for sale. I believe I'm owed something for what I've done for the family and the company."

"May I ask, what do you believe you are owed?"

"Of course you can ask, Preacher. I'll tell you what I am owed!" Spike's blue eyes narrow toward mine before he continues, "I'm owed a share of the profit. I've helped build the business into what it is today. Has he told you all that I've done for the business? Or has he just said I had my share of the family business and inheritance back in my twenties when I took off with my college money, and blew it all? That now I have no title or claim to anything related to Cornelius Printing?"

Spike stabs a three-tiered square of pancakes, and the gesture reveals the line on his wrist where the tattoo extends up his shirt sleeve, and glares at me with angry eyes, waiting for a reply. While he chomps his breakfast, I check myself not to take the bait. No need to use argument to counter his flash of anger. I use a sip of coffee to pause then quietly respond.

"Spike, for the next few moments, I don't really care about what Reggie has said. I care about what you have to say, your story. I realize that I've buried your father and now, more recently, your mother. While I know a good bit about the other members of your family, I really know very little about you.

"I've learned that you are very active in the Holy Trinity Community Church. I know you work at Cornelius. I know, or at least I think I know, that your father loved you very much, as did your mother. Beyond that, I don't know much more. But I believe there is much more to learn. I'd like to hear your story. How did Spike get to where he is today? Your brother says you are extremely bright and very talented in ways that astound him."

"Oh, I wouldn't say I astound him. I probably confound him, particularly now, sticking my nose into the sale of his business."

He speaks with less tension in his voice, smiling before he takes another forkful of pancakes, followed by an oversized piece of country ham. He takes a moment to chew, and a sip of coffee. I sense he is calculating just how far he wants to share his life's story with his brother's pastor. He uses the final piece of pancake to swipe the last of the maple syrup from his plate and, finishing that bite, places his fork and knife in the ten o'clock position to signal to the server he is done with his meal. I watch to see if he is finished with the conversation, as well.

"It's a long story, Jon. I can call you Jon, right?"

"Please."

"And it's not a pretty story, but it is what it is."

Gladys, our server gathers the cleaned platters as Spike fills first mine, and then his cup with coffee from the table decanter.

"I guess you could say I was the family prodigal son. You can get that, can't you, Jon?"

My widened eyes and gentle nod convey I am with him in the metaphor.

"I did some very stupid and selfish things in my early twenties. And it is true—I did demand my share of my college funds. I didn't know until sometime later that those college funds my parents had put away for Reggie and myself were all that my parents had for an estate. They had nothing but the business for any retirement plan. But I demanded what had been put aside in my name and I took off. Left town. Blew it all in a stupid start-up of a tattoo shop, which quickly went bust. Fell into bad company. I created a fan club of losers. Then, my money ran out!

"I got into alcohol and drugs in a bad way. Looking back, I don't remember half of that time, except that I ended up broke and sick. Thought and felt like I was going to die. My counselors said I came close.

"Anyway, to make the story shorter, I ended up in a faith-based rehab program, part of my sentence for drunken behavior and possession of narcotics. Bounced in and out of that program, recycled a few times, before it took. But eventually, I got clean for good, been sober now for nine years, ten months, and two days. I know now that I can take one drink or shoot up just once and I will be back into full-blown stoned. So, for me, it's just one day at a time. Has been all these years. Just one day at a time."

Spike's pause appears to offer him a moment of reflection as he takes another sip. Continuing to look into his cup, he starts again.

"While in rehab, I started back to school, online, and eventually finished a degree in graphic arts and marketing. I worked a handful of jobs across South Georgia and into Florida, the Jacksonville area. I wanted to come home, but was too ashamed. Eventually, I swallowed my shame and came back to see Mom and Dad. They both insisted that I stay, and I did. Dad let me go back into his shop and created a job for me.

"I found God during those cycles in rehab, but when I went to church with them, where I had grown up, The Hill, I just didn't seem to fit. I was uncomfortable, and I felt all the classy city folks were uncomfortable with me, as well. I found a sense of home at Holy Trinity, where I met my wife, and her two kids. I became a family man.

"Worked steady at the printing company. Eventually, I suggested to Dad and Reggie that I could bring in some business if they would give me a try. Reggie didn't believe me, but Dad overruled him and let me have a half-dozen accounts to service. They were low-end accounts, not much risk if they were lost. But within three years, the revenue from those six accounts doubled and through referrals, I added another two dozen accounts. Before Dad died, the revenue for Cornelius had doubled in the time he gave me those first accounts, and at least seventy-five percent of that growth could be attributed to the accounts and new customers I served or brought in."

Looking up to read my eyes, he takes a deep breath and continues.

"In the time between Dad's death and now Mom's passing, our revenue has doubled again. That might not sound like much, but is unbelievable in the printing industry today. According to the latest data, the printing industry as a whole has been flat across the country. Only a few companies have grown, mostly by buy-outs of smaller companies like ours. Over forty-five percent of the small to medium printing shops have gone out of business since 2001.

"I'm probably boring you, aren't I?"

"Absolutely not, keep going. This is fascinating." I realize my curiosity is piqued.

"Jon, here's the bottom line on this matter of me sticking my nose in my brother's chance to sell the business: I believe I am a big part of the reason there is a business to sell, and a business that has a handsome profit to boot!"

Spike glances up over my head at the grimy, faded, Royal Crown neon clock on the wall behind our booth, then double-checks the time on his watch and quickly signals Gladys for the check.

"Got to go, Jon. I have a deadline production for the Coupon Mailer in two hours. I hope this is helpful. I might have already said too much for my own good, but I just have to trust you."

He reaches for the check, but I cover it with my hand ahead of him.

"This is on me, Spike. Thank you so much for your time. As I suspected, there are several sides to this issue, and I thank you for letting me hear your side."

"No problem, Jon. See you around."

Spike spins out of our booth and halfway toward the front door before I turn over the check to see the damages and calculate the tip I will leave Gladys.

CHAPTER SEVENTEEN

As scheduled during our meeting last week, Dr. Dan and I re-connect this Monday morning. I bring him up-to-date on the progress being made on the project as I had outlined in the proposal. I also give him a thumbnail sketch of my meeting with Max and my follow-up visit with Spike. Dr. Dan applauds these developments and that lifts my spirits.

"Jon, this is a good start. If you recall in our visit over your current proposal, I admitted that the direction you were taking in this matter of business and faith was also new territory for me, as well. So, I've been exploring the subject among my colleagues here at Conley, and one professor in particular is quite interested in your subject and wants to talk. You remember Dr. Nicholas Kostopoulos?"

"Yes, I took one DMin class he co-chaired. I believe Dr. K's focus was Ethics."

"That's right. His PhD from Harvard is in Christian Ethics, but he also holds another PhD in Economics, from the University of Chicago. He is very interested in your proposal and wants to talk with you. I think he would be a great resource for helping you to fine-tune your ideas. He suggests you call him and set up a time to get together. Sooner will be better than later as he is headed to Brazil on a sabbatical in about two months."

"Thanks, Dr. Dan. I'll pursue this right away. Talk to you next week."

Within the hour, I place a call and receive confirmation for a meeting over lunch with Dr. Kostopoulos on Thursday. This timing will work well for me, as I will be in the area for Gladys Millsap's bypass cardiovascular surgery at Emory Hospital that day.

We meet as planned in the cafeteria of the student center. Dr. K arrives late at the cafeteria entrance, his five-foot frame clothed in a rumpled hounds-tooth brown plaid jacket, baggy wrinkled khaki tan pants that have no memory of a crease, and a black T-shirt. His thick glasses framed in hard, black oversized plastic make his eyes appear pinpointed, way too small for his big head of curly black and silver hair. His bushy mustache blends in with his five-o'clock shadow. He is hungry and quickly ushers me into the line passing in front of the display of chilled salads and steaming soups. We concentrate on getting food quickly, then seated, with the least amount of conversation as possible. I soon rediscover how difficult it is to understand Dr. K's dialogue. I study his shrouded lips and listen intently to find the English code hidden in his heavy Greek accent.

"Dr. Dan tells me you are diving into the matter of business and faith in your DMin project. Tell me what you hope to do." Dr. K is quick to get to the point.

I expected this request and I eagerly reply.

"I hope to develop a greater understanding of how the two fields connect so I can be a better minister to my members, particularly those who are in business. I think I am clueless as to what they experience, what really bothers them. I feel like I am missing something. Or they are missing something. I suspect that in most of my sermons, they are like Charlie Brown in the school classroom, hearing nothing from his teacher but, 'Wah waaah wah wah waaahhh wah!'"

Dr. K has a puzzled look on his face, having missed my illustration.

I realize I have just failed to communicate again, and restate.

"It seems to me that I have been speaking a lot of piety from the pulpit that has little connection with the tough issues facing the people in the pews. I'd like to change that, if I can. Perhaps you can help me."

"Ah-ha. So, now I understand. You don't understand your people who are in business, and the people in business don't understand you! No?"

"Yes, you might say that is the heart of matter. That's what I'm trying to correct as my DMin project. Can you help me?"

"Maybe so. Can't make any promises, but maybe so. Do you have an idea of where to start?"

"Well, I remember in one of your lectures a while back you talked about a passage in Psalms, the phrase,

'I will lift up mine eyes unto the hills,
from whence cometh my help.
My help cometh from the Lord,
who made heaven and earth.'

"That passage and your explanation made a profound impression on me. If I remember correctly, you explained that the passage was not an affirmation of the hills as a source of inspiration, but just the opposite. The source of inspiration was from God, not the hills. And the poet was making a contrast to the way the farmers around him worshipped the god of fertility represented in the hills, with offerings and sexual activity with the prostitutes in those hills. The Psalmist was pressing for the alternative approach to the matter of fertile crops, complete reliance on Yahweh as their sole source of life."

"My, my, you did listen. And…" Dr. K responds with an open pregnant pause.

I continue.

"I have never looked at mountains the same way since. But I have also pondered just how much I am missing in other parts of Scripture where there are implications of business, or rather agriculture, and how the faith of the Hebrews speaks to the integration of the two.

"I've been digging a little deeper on the subject, particularly around the person and teachings of Amos, and realize I have overlooked many other possibilities beyond Amos."

Now, I play the pause.

"Jon, you make me proud. You are right on target. Amos is a good example, but just one of many, where the content of the Scripture is loaded with economic and business issues that we just gloss over every day. So, here's my question—how far do you want to go in this research? I've spent the better part of forty years studying the triangulation of religion, economics, and ethics and I could go on and on, as what is it you just said? ...'wah waaahh waaahhh wah wah!'"

We both laugh out loud.

"Dr. K, I don't want to be a professor of ethics and economics. I'll leave that to you. But I would like to make a real connection between faith and the business world. I am beginning to feel that it is sort of a calling. I don't want to be the professor, just the practitioner, if you know what I mean."

"Got it. I would say the place to start is Scripture—you've already scratched the surface here. Most theologians—well, let me qualify that before I get on the academic rack—*some* theologians, and to a larger extent most pastors and preachers, and Bible teachers, never look for and therefore do not see any business connection in the Scripture they read or teach their students. It is there and most always completely overlooked. And then people are shocked when you point out these connections. They think you are some kind of demon for pointing out something that is less than the devotional mumbo-jumbo I see so much of.

"For example, most people remember the story of Joseph, particularly his childhood, and his rise to fame with Pharaoh, but hardly anyone recognizes or admits that he was one of antiquity's earliest examples of a hedge fund operator. He actually 'bet the farm,' so to speak in your Americanism, that the 'market' was going to fail. If he had been wrong, he would have turned out to be a fool of the Bible rather than a big hero.

"He correctly read the cycles and trends of the rise and fall of a series of bountiful harvests offset by a series of crop failures and famines. He used the history of these rises and falls to predict—accurately, in fact—that the good times his pharaoh ruler enjoyed would eventually come to an end followed by a famine. He bet accurately that crops that were cheap because they were so bountiful would become extremely valuable and pricey if they could be saved for a period when the inevitable famine cycle arrived. If you bought while it was cheap, held it, put it away in silos, then waited for the bad times, you could make a killing in the market because the scarcity of the grain would then sell at a premium to the highest bidder. The highest bidder could be your own countrymen, or your neighboring realm. Decades after Joseph was sold away by his brothers, the father and the brothers experienced total crop failure, a life-threatening famine. The only food available was in Egypt, under Joseph's silos, and thus they had to make their way to Egypt to buy the grain at any price in order to survive.

"Now, some folks say that was not fair, not Christian! Joseph should have given it away. Some even say Joseph sold his own people into slavery over this imbalance of commodities. But the point is Joseph was a hustler and a strategist. He wasn't a magician, but an early trader in commodities. Not the pretty picture we always want to see. Kind of taints our version of our childhood Sunday school stories of Joseph the victim turned saint.

"So, to your point, Jon. Think about the next time you have this story of Joseph show up in the Scripture you are reading. You use the lectionary, right?"

"Yes," I nod. "Quite regularly now, though I don't make a big deal out of it. I just do it. It helps me keep away from my favorite texts and forces me to deal with things I might want to avoid."

"Precisely, Jon, and here is the point. Think about the next time the story of Joseph comes up in the lectionary, and you read it that Sunday. Suppose you took the time to show this side of Joseph, Joseph the hedge fund operator. Now, you might not find a wonderful theology in that fact, but for the first time you just might get the attention of the business people in your audience, the woman in the pew who just lost a bundle in the market because her hedge fund went south based on the advice of her 'can't lose' stock picker, for example. I could go on and on about business issues that Jacob faced and addressed as an entrepreneur. The money changer that Jesus tossed out of the temple, the fierce concern about inheritance, land rights, fair wages, interest, bank loans. Over and over again, it is there, business rubbing up against religion and vice-versa."

"Wow, never thought of those possibilities. But I see your point."

"And furthermore, Jon, the history of the Church—or, for that matter, before the Church, to the history of Judaism as an institution—if you look for it, you can find this tug of war between the business world and Judaism, or capitalism and socialism and the Church. Wherever you look, if you look deep enough, you will see currents and undercurrents of business. So, in the moment I have left to finish my coconut cream pie before running off to my next class, what I would say is two things:

"First, keep your eyes and mind open to the possibilities of these connections of religion, economics, and ethics and be willing to share your puzzlement or your understanding with the people you serve, the business people. They will appreciate your honesty and curiosity.

"Second, I suggest there is one other avenue you might travel in your research, and that is the area of redaction criticism. I've shared your thoughts with Dr. Dave Gilliam. He is an expert in redaction criticism. Give him a call, set up a time to meet with him. I think you both would enjoy the conversation, particularly in the vein of how redaction and business play together. I'll send you an email with his contact info. Got to run. Peace, my friend, and good luck."

My thoughts are awash in all the affirmation and insight I have just received. I arrive in the surgical waiting room and am greeted by somber faces of the Milsap family. Gladys' recovery from surgery has developed complications, and she will remain in intensive care for the remainder of the week. I pray with the family and hope that the outcome will be positive. I promise to be back, often, to check on them and on Gladys when she can have visitors.

CHAPTER EIGHTEEN

The next morning, I honor my dental appointment for an annual check-up and, since the dental office is only four blocks down from the Pine Grove Nursing Home and Rehab Center, I check on three members of the congregation who reside there. By the time I leave Pine Grove, it is mid-morning and hunger pangs remind me that I skipped breakfast as my contribution to a dental hygiene exam. I stop by the Tic Toc to get a quick serving of their fried eggs with corned beef hash. I take a back booth, order, and while sipping coffee review my iPhone calendar.

Roy Croaker slips quietly into the other side of the booth.

"Good morning, Rev. It's been a while since I've had your company for breakfast. School year and kids catching the bus tying up your mornings?"

"Yeah, Roy, something like that. Sorry for being a slacker. The doc put me on warning that I needed to watch the cholesterol, and I've been behaving myself with oatmeal most mornings. Just had a hankering for your eggs and corn beef hash this morning and actually had a moment to grab some. How have you been doing? How's business?"

"Same ole, same ole, you know." Roy nudges back his ever-present white cap with no visor. "Running this place twenty-four-seven is a non-stop challenge. I'd have to say I'm the one slacking lately. Haven't been to church in months. Been looking for a weekend manager to get myself some relief and time with the family, but so far, no luck. Good managers, honest managers, are hard to come by. You know anyone who wants to manage a 24-hour diner every weekend?"

"Afraid I can't help you there, Roy. But I have been missing you. Other than keeping the community fed at all hours of the night, what else have you been up to?"

"That's it. It's all I can handle right now. I bought a place down on the lake, nice little cottage with a dock, on a private cove. Bought it almost a year ago, spent only three weekends there since then. Probably wasted my money, but my wife wanted it for the family, particularly the kids. They've enjoyed it some, but I've been tied down here."

"Roy, you need to watch yourself, take care of yourself, for you and for your family. Helen told me last Sunday that the doc is concerned about your heart. She said you have some history of heart attacks in your family and you're not taking care of yourself."

"Yeah, you're right. I'm looking into the heart thing. Thinking about stopping smoking, but not quite there yet." Roy pauses to redirect the conversation away from him and his health. "By the way, there's been some talk around here among the regulars about your sermon a few weeks back. Something about being more concerned about business people. That true?"

"Might be. What have you heard?"

"That you want to see how some of our businesses work. You want to listen to us and learn our concerns. Are you sure you're not getting ready to run for city council? If you are, I'd vote for you, not because you have any experience in business, but just because I like you."

"Well, thanks, Roy. I appreciate your honesty and your support. I like you, too. I guess some of what you're hearing is correct. I am interested in the daily lives of the people I care about, including you. I'm not interested in telling anyone how to run their businesses. But I really am interested in how business owners face daily challenges and what I might learn from them that will help me help them. Take the Tic Toc here. It is one of the busiest places and longest-running establishments in town. I eat here occasionally, chat with you from time to time, but I really don't have a clue what you're up against with this business. Maybe you would like to fill me in. If you would, I'd like to learn."

"Here are your eggs and hash. On me. You are right on one account, Jon. I never thought any pastor in our town cared two hoots about my business other than trying to make me close it down on Sundays. But I don't know what to tell you. Running the Tic Toc is more than just pulling raw food in, fixing it so it's edible, and serving it hot or cold and getting paid for it. It's not that simple. But most people think it is. Everybody thinks they can run a restaurant, that it's a no-brainer cash machine. But look around town. Six restaurants have opened in the last three years and all but one of them have gone bankrupt. And the word on the street is that the sixth one is on slippery ground with accounts payable over ninety days old.

"Customers complain when prices go up and when the service starts to slip when I'm short of help. But other than that, the average diner doesn't give a damn about what it takes to make this place run non-stop. The closest thing I have to someone listening to me about my problems other than my wife and my accountant are the wholesale guys who drop in every week, steady as clockwork to get my orders for the coming week. But they don't really care when fifty pounds of bacon disappears out the back door. Hell, they think it's good for their business. And they sure as hell can't help me find a short-order cook and replace a waitress who's off having a baby."

As I lap up the sticky remains off my platter with a corner of rye toast, I let Roy's words sink in a moment before I respond.

"Roy, how would you like to change just a little bit what you have just described?"

"What do you mean, Rev?"

"Someone to listen, like other business people or even your pastor."

"Well, the first sounds like a commercial set-up for getting me to renew my membership to the Chamber of Commerce. The second? Having my pastor's ear on my business stuff? Never considered it. Tell me more."

"What if the church came to you? What if I met with you, maybe a few other business people, weekly or bi-weekly, and we just had down-to-earth, no-holds-barred conversations about the challenges you face in business. Would you be interested?"

"Depends. I kind of like keeping my business problems to myself, and so would most of the business people I know in town. So, I'm not keen on airing the dirty laundry of the Tic Toc. Not too keen on hearing the same of other businesses, either."

"I understand. Perhaps I didn't phrase it in the best way. Suppose you had a chance to push back on some of the things I say without repercussions. Suppose we made our conversation more like a dialogue and not a sermon. Suppose we got down to admitting what really seems unreasonable when it comes to religious teachings and discuss those matters. Would you be game?"

"Maybe. Tell me more."

"One of the ideas I have is for business people like you to get together with me, and do two things. One thing we would do is let you talk and you give me your honest feedback about what I said in a previous sermon—with complete freedom. The other thing we would do is to look over some Scriptures that I plan to preach on, and you and your buddies tell me what it is about that Scripture that bothers you. Does that sound appealing?"

"Sounds scary, if I'm you and I tell you what I really think. Not so sure you would be ready for my comments. Might shock you."

"And they might. But I'm willing to try it if you are. What do you say?"

"Okay. So, tell me how this might work. We sit around like we're in an AA meeting, but instead of it being alcohol, it's a bunch of workaholics?" Roy adds with a chuckle. "I'm Roy, and I'm a workaholic. I am slowly killing myself and ruining my family. I'm helpless and can't do anything about it except just take one day at a time."

We both laugh at that.

"Roy, here's what I'm thinking. I'd like you to consider hosting a gathering of your business colleagues for an early-morning breakfast in your back room to explore this idea. We would pay for our meals and the extra gratuity. But you would hang with us during that time, be part of the discussion. How does that sound so far?"

"I'd like the business. Probably like the company, depending on who shows up. But I don't want to be in charge. I'll be in my whites and dirty apron, and might have to respond to a crisis in the kitchen. But I'd give it a try. When do you want to start?"

"In about ten days or two weeks. I'll give you plenty of advance notice, and you can help me set the best time for you. I know the morning Rotary club meets on Thursday for breakfast, so what about Tuesday mornings? 7 a.m.? Would that work for the Tic Toc?"

"We'll just make it work. Let me know."

We shake hands and part, Roy back into the kitchen revving up for the daily blue plate specials, me heading back to my study at The Hill, pondering along the way what my next move will be. Who will I invite? Who will accept? And who will actually show up to this gathering idea of mine?

CHAPTER NINETEEN

O ver the next three days, I learn more about Gladys' condition: that she suffered a mild stroke during the surgery, and her condition is stable, but no visitation. Since Gladys and several of her family members are members of the Chancel Choir, I ask Bryan to step in and cover the daily hospital visits until I can return there on Friday.

Meanwhile, as Dr. K suggested, I call Dr. Gilliam, introduce myself, and arrange to meet him for lunch in the same student cafeteria. I remember Dr. Gilliam's writings from my time at seminary, having read some of his textbooks. He is a nationally recognized New Testament professor and author of several commentaries, some of which are quite controversial. In the more conservative circles of several denominations, Dr. Gilliam has been accused of being a heretic for his participation in *The Jesus Scholars,* a voluntary gathering of experts in biblical criticism who periodically meet in order to discuss their differing opinions on the true source of many of the sayings attributed to Jesus in the Gospel accounts.

In the days between meeting Dr. K and contacting Dr. Gilliam, I have brushed up on my redaction criticism. I remember it from seminary days as one of the various methods of examining ancient texts of the Scriptures. In the seminary setting, the objective was to pass the exam about the distinctions between historical criticism, text criticism, literary criticism, and redaction criticism. After the passing grade, the distinctions between those methods of biblical interpretation gradually faded away.

I arrive at the entrance to the student center cafeteria a bit nervous at the prospect of having lunch with such a prominent scholar and controversial character. The only image I have of this man is the thumbnail portrait on the cover of his latest publication, *Revisiting the Gospel's Audience… for Today's Application.* I didn't have time to read it, but I did take a few moments to skim the summary on Amazon just before I clicked "Buy Now." The book will not arrive for another three days.

I notice a person with features similar but much older that the portrait on the book cover. I approach the gentleman carefully.

"Dr. Gilliam?"

"You must be Jonathan Boatwright. Good to meet you. Nick has spoken highly of you and the work you are doing. Shall we get something to eat? I'm starving!"

As soon as we are seated with our trays, Dr. Gilliam begins to eat his meal immediately without pausing to offer a prayer, and I follow his example. Between bites of dull, routine student center cuisine, we exchange some cursory background information as a way to get to know each other. In a matter of moments, the conversation turns to the purpose of our meeting.

Dr. Gilliam begins. "Nick tells me that the focus of your doctoral work is the intersection of faith and business. I don't know whether to commend you on being a very brave pastor or have a touch of pity for your venture into areas that can be full of surprises and consternation."

"I think I am getting in touch with the need for both," I reply and go further. "Dr. K believes your work in redaction criticism can be a valuable resource for me as I try to create a bridge between the pulpit and the pew, or to put it more precisely, the business community. I must confess that I am a bit rusty on redaction, and I have not had the chance to read your latest publication, *Revisiting the Gospels' Audience*—I just ordered it and look forward to its arrival in a few days."

"Ah, I finished that two years ago and the publisher is just now getting around to releasing it. However, one of the chapters, if I recall, focuses on the business and economic issues facing the congregations of the early church. Redaction, if you will recall from your seminary days, is looking at collections of writings and determining what the editors attempted to address. Why were some writings preserved and others lost?

"Redaction, I like to tell my students, is like downsizing in a major move. Unfortunately, most of my students are "upsizing" as they try to advance their careers and don't always get what I mean. But as you get older and are looking at retirement, you begin to look around at all you have collected over the years and realize a lot of it is just junk, just stuff. Some of it was good when you got it, maybe even cherished. But as the years pass, and your needs change, you find you don't use some things as often as others. So, as in the case of seniors who need to relocate to a smaller scale of living, you have to sort through life's junk and decide what to keep, what to toss—what has helped you in the past is less important than what helps you live today.

"As you might imagine, I have accumulated thousands of books, and my wife has put her foot down and said you can have one wall of bookshelves, one wall only, in the new condo we are moving to. She has, in effect, given me an ultimatum, requiring me to sort through thousands of books and arrive at a few hundred that will fit comfortably in those new shelves. So, over the next few months, I will select the volumes that have meant the most to me, and that I expect to continue to value in my future reading until my dying day.

"That, Jon, is a metaphor of what happened in the selection of the stories we have in the Gospels today. In other words, after several decades following Jesus, there were thousands of stories collected about what he did and what he said. Over time, the stories that stuck, that really mattered, were the stories that addressed the needs of the congregation at the time of editing, many decades later. Therefore, what we see in the collection of the four Gospels are the stories and teachings that were most helpful then—not in the time of Jesus, but in the first century of the church, the gathering of those who called themselves Christians, or followers of Jesus."

Dr. Gilliam pauses to sip his iced tea and take a bite of cookie, then continues.

"In that chapter of my latest book about business, I argue, to the distress of many of my colleagues, that we can see over and over again that business, money, prosperity, and estates were all big issues in the early church. We tend to think that the church was a huddled mass of only poor people put upon by the oppressive governments wherever those churches might be gathered. Indeed, the gospel message was attractive to the poor, but it was also attractive to the rich and to the business people.

"Two things were happening in the early church. They had poor people, and there were probably a few who felt empowered, looking to get their act together and climb out of poverty. Some members, once dirt-poor and powerless, were now self-sufficient, and eventually became leaders in the community, particularly the church community. But you also had the wealthy, the business professionals like tax collectors and debt collectors, traders, bankers, who also listened to the Jesus story and realized they needed more than money and power in their lives. They were facing mid-life crises with nowhere to turn for answers. Folks seeking answers to life's questions are coming into the church at various stages of wealth and personal development, and the church is struggling with what to do with them. So, it is the stories of Jesus that speak to these issues, real-life issues, with real-life illustrations, that are collected and retold, over and over again, to address issues that seem to repeat themselves each generation and in each gathered community of believers. These stories became so effective, they were remembered and become part of the official record of Jesus and eventually canonized as Scripture.

"So, I argue that today, we seem to have this crazy avoidance of addressing business and wealth—except when it comes to trying to get the rich to give the church some money so the church can build a big cathedral or a seminary and pay a staff to run its institutions. And pay me, as well—I have to confess. The only note we seem to be playing in the church when it comes to wealth, or business, or money, is stewardship, which the average person in the pew interprets to mean making a pledge or giving a tithe."

I take a sip of tea and interject an observation. "I confess that I'm guilty of that. You're hitting a nerve."

"Jon, I'm a seminary professor, not a priest." Dr. Gilliam chuckles, offers a sign of the cross, then adds, "But I accept your confession and offer my limited absolution. You are one of the few pastors who are beginning to explore the practical intersection of faith and good business practices."

"Wow, Dr. Gilliam. That's great to hear. Can you give me some examples in the Gospels that illustrate your argument? I'm sure you address them in your book I'm about to read, but I'd like to hear it from you."

"Sure. It is not such a stretch of the imagination to see the early church starting to receive folks who are already successful in their business life. They like this notion of grace and forgiveness for everyone, including them. But they come to the church with their questions that had been answered previously in the civil or religious courts. Sticky stuff, complicated stuff. For example, inheritance is a huge thing, then and now.

"Suppose you are an heir to a fortune, and you want to join this group called Christians, but your benefactors aren't dead yet and will disown you if you follow this radical group. You have few choices. You can postpone your endorsement of this group until after your benefactors have died, take your inheritance, do with it as you wish, and sign up later for the Jesus movement when it's all gone. Or, you can sign away your inheritance now, and get on with following Jesus. Today, this would be like persons who postpone a commitment to Jesus until they have retired with a nice plan and THEN have the freedom to become a 'volunteer.'

"Another example: Imagine the early church in some form of a business meeting and a sub-committee raises the issue of membership—Jerome, everyone knows Jerry, he's the unofficial IRS guy, who rips off people and buys their tax refund ahead of time but with a huge discount, and sometimes forgets to file that return. The committee reports that Jerry has suddenly got 'religion' and wants to join the group. Half of the congregation wants to see if he has really changed, and the other half are ready to fry him, angry at his past behavior which has cost them each a small fortune. The case goes to the elders, who debate this back and forth for a long time, until someone calls for the old guy named Luke, now in his nineties, to see if he has any suggestions. He is the local expert about the teachings of Jesus.

"Luke, from his memory of stories handed down to him, tells the elders the story of Zacchaeus, which hopefully sets the stage for the behavior of the congregation. Zacchaeus is welcomed into the fold, to have communion with them, BEFORE he makes any changes in his behavior. This overture of grace breaks down and overwhelms Zacchaeus whose response is emotional and practical—he takes unbelievable initiative to correct the situation. They, the early church, hear this story, try it out in their situation, and it works. So they keep the story, and they keep Jerome."

"Now, we have to be careful in our use of redaction, not to force our own objectives into the Gospel accounts to mirror our current goal or belief. But there is a great benefit from the practical application of the Gospel in twenty-first-century life, if we could see that their original intent may have been to convert sinners to saints. However, we could also argue that the Gospels became the handbook for how to handle common situations in the days of the early church.

"Now, Jon, I've got to run to class, but before I go, I must warn you. This approach will be tough for some to accept, and it could get you in a lot of trouble very quickly, particularly among some literalist viewpoints. Call me if I can be of help. Move slowly in this matter. Get comfortable with the concept as it applies to you, before you launch into making it apply to anyone else. Nice talking to you, got to go. You're on the right track. Stay strong, be of good courage. Peace!" And Dr. Gilliam darts off to his class, already five minutes late.

With the cafeteria quickly emptying, I remain at the table and note the high points of Dr. Gilliam's conversation on my tablet. The examples he gave me inspire me, but I ponder longest over the parting advice. Getting comfortable with the concept as it applies to me might be my biggest challenge.

CHAPTER TWENTY

O nly when I pull into The Hill parking lot do I remember the promise I made to the Nelson family. There they are, the husband George sitting in the driver's seat, his hand extended out the side window flipping the ashes from his cigarette, the wife—what was her name?—leans forward into the side opening of the mostly dull-grey Dodge Caravan with corrosive, rusting quarter panels outlining the well-worn tires. She seems to be changing a diaper for the youngest child whom I remember being about eight months old. The elementary-age twins are chasing each other around the parking lot, an older child I do not remember seeing yesterday sits on the curb bordering the sidewalk, her skinny arms wrap around her knees, which are drawn up under her chin. George approached me yesterday in the parking lot as Rusty and I prepared to leave the church and head home for Sunday lunch.

George has a familiar story—passing through town on the way to Florida to pick citrus, their money depleted, no gas, no food, no place to stay, and no diapers. Could the pastor give them some money to get on down the road?

I am accustomed to these after-church approaches in the parking lot, a scene that often feels deliberately staged so as to put the pastor on the spot. Yesterday afternoon, I had gone into autopilot with the

Nelsons and used the policy of the church, set up long before my arrival— never to give cash to anyone who sought assistance.

When I had interviewed for the position of senior pastor of The Hill, an attractive feature was its commitment to help the needy in the community in practical ways. I was impressed with the system that was in place. The church office had an arrangement with the Mountain View Motel, owned and operated by the Patel family, to accept any family we sent over. Mountain View required only a fifty-dollar nightly rate billed to the church. Since the office was already closed yesterday afternoon when George had approached me, I had called ahead and made the arrangements with the Patels for the Nelsons to spend the night on Sunday. I also had arranged through another standing agreement with the Tic Toc for the family to have dinner and breakfast. The diner is supposed to request reimbursement from the church, but never does. As I turned off the ignition, I tried to anticipate my next step with the Nelson family. George, now standing outside the van, leans with his back against the driver's door of the Caravan, his arms crossed and head down and waits for my approach.

"Good morning, Mr. Nelson. Did you get a good night's sleep and something to eat?"

"Yes, Pastor Boatwright. Thanks very much. It was really nice to have a hot shower and good bed for a change. We had a good dinner, and a good breakfast, thanks to you."

We eye each other and pause to see who would continue the conversation. George waits for me to take the lead, and I wait to see what he wants next. He blinks first.

"You mentioned something yesterday about getting us some gas for the van so we could get on down the road today."

"Yes, I did. I'll give you some directions for that in just a minute." My eyes glance to the left, searching the van's front tire for treads and detecting none. "How far do you have to go to get to your job?"

"We'll try to make Valdosta tonight. I have some folks down that way who might be able to put us up, then we'll try to make Plant City by Wednesday and catch up with my brother. We would really appreciate anything you can do to help us."

"I think we can help you with a tank of gas. Joe's Exxon is two blocks south on Main Street. I'll go in now and call ahead for you." I extend my hand to George, and he responds in kind. "May I offer a prayer for your safe journey, George?"

With his nod granting acceptance, I ask God's travel mercies upon the Nelson family and their safe arrival today in South Georgia and good job prospects in Florida tomorrow. George adds his Amen at the end, then quickly calls the twins to get in the van with their mother and two sisters. I watch them pull out of the parking lot before I head into the office, where I ask Elizabeth to call Joe and provide gas for the Nelson family, in a grey van, with New York plates. I already know what will follow: Joe will present the family with a coupon for two buckets of chicken and all the fixings at the Chick'n Hut next door—Joe's other business venture— all part of the quiet system of benevolence, which makes me proud of the community I serve.

It has been several weeks since a Nelson-type family has presented their needs to me or some other member of the congregation. It seems to come in waves, the highest frequency during the change of seasons, when migration from north to south or vice versa follows the harvest seasons along the East Coast. Doing something good for the neediest in the world is the part of ministry that warms my soul. When I pondered the possibility that someday I might be a pastor, I envisioned preaching messages of love and care, recruiting people and resources to provide practical solutions—for the strangers passing through the area, or the mother of small children fleeing from their abusive home.

The Hill is noted for its benevolence. No small wonder that it seems to receive a high volume of requests for assistance. The word is out in the community; this church really cares for people down on their luck. When it comes to the community pantry, the largest pool of volunteers from any one church come from this church, as well as the largest collection of non-perishable food items. Youth mission trips to places like Haiti and rural Mexico include personal delivery of clothing the church collects. A rotating system of summer missions, local one year, another site somewhere in the US the next year, and the third year a mission project somewhere beyond the borders, provide a local-to-global response to human need. I am proud of The Hill, and glad to be its senior pastor.

I settle down to my desk with my usual morning coffee as Elizabeth places Saturday's and Monday's mail on the right corner of the desk, and spears the pink phone call messages onto the spindle next to the phone. I quickly flip through the bundle of mail, mostly flyers and offers for books, movies, web designs for churches, stewardship campaigns, and next year's Vacation Bible School curriculum, all of which go directly to the trash can with no more than a glance. I do read a letter thanking me for my recent work with the Wintergreen Hospice Butterfly Release Memorial Service. I appreciate this and add it to the junk mail pile. Two note cards, one thanks me for my service to the Cornelius family for my pastoral care and funeral service—what a wonderful job I did. The second note comes from Max Maximillian, who thanks me for my time in the ride-around. Both are reassuring. They find their temporary storage in the bottom right-hand desk drawer, wedged in among the other cards and thank you notes that I habitually accumulate. Remembering that these expressions of gratitude are there, filling the drawer to capacity, is enough to help me through the situations where I feel my services or practical help are severely lacking.

Next, I turn my attention to the messages, and sort them by urgency. Elizabeth is usually pretty good at this and after scanning the entire stack of twelve, I return to the top: *Molly Squires—704-274-4433— Bill lost his job! Please call ASAP!*

"Hello, Molly, this is Jon. Got your message that you called, something about Bill and his job."

I listen as Molly talks softly, as to not be overheard, explaining that Bill has been let go from his job in Atlanta. She discovered this only last evening when Bill confessed to faking his going to work for three weeks, too embarrassed to tell her. This week's paycheck is from his severance package and will be their last. Bill is downstairs now, watching reruns of yesterday's playoff games, drinking pretty heavily, and not talking, just staring at the screen, sipping beer all night and into this morning. He hasn't bathed or shaved or eaten anything since Friday evening. Her voice and her pauses reveal her panic about what Bill might do to himself.

He is fifty-eight years old, has been with that company for the past twelve years. He says he has been looking for work every day since he was abruptly terminated, escorted by security out the door with only his box of personal items and a letter of termination. He's not the only one, he says; four others in his department got the ax, as well. They have been hanging out together at Bud's Grill every day trying to figure out what to do next. With that, I promise to drop by the house after lunch.

Unemployment is not my pastoral forte. Present me with a transient family packed into a van without fuel, food, or shelter and I can dive in to do whatever can be done to get them on their way. As we've seen, The Hill has systems in place that can respond with Biblical hospitality— even prescriptions filled and billed to the church at Park's Pharmacy as well as clothing at the Goodwill. But unemployment! I have never experienced that crisis, nor do I have any training. I know from my Clinical Pastoral Experience internship at the hospital how to work with the sick, the injured, the terminally ill. What do I have to offer to someone like Bill?

He is not the first unemployment crisis I have encountered. There have been others, and now I am beginning to recall my own feelings of helplessness dealing with those situations as I make my way to visit Molly and Bill. As I shuffle my Ford through mid-afternoon traffic toward the Squires' home in Millsboro, a small village south of town, I realize I cannot recall anything about Bill's job, what he did, who he worked for, where he worked. Bill and Molly just show up semi-regularly, about twice a month—nice folks, regular givers it seems, two daughters previously active in the youth church, now beyond college, one married (I officiated), the other off somewhere in a job out of state. I try to recall what Molly does. Was she a homemaker, or did she have a career? I conclude that she does not work outside the home—evidenced by her presence at home on Monday morning when we spoke by phone.

When I turn onto Vernon Drive, a Johnson County Sheriff Deputy car blocks my path. A stern-faced female uniformed officer approaches me and explains the road is blocked except for emergency vehicles. Looking beyond the deputy's car, I can detect flashing red lights of multiple emergency and rescue vehicles idling a half block down, just in front of the Squires' home. My stomach does a flip and, with my heart in my throat, I explain that I am the pastor of the Squires family and ask what happened.

"Can't say, sir. Do you have some identification?"

I produce my driver's license along with a photo Clergy Pass badge issued by the Mountain View Health Systems, which I nervously retrieve from the console. The deputy moves in front of my car and uses her shoulder mic to communicate to another source and returns the IDs.

"Rev. Boatwright, you can go ahead. An officer will meet you at the residence."

My innards turn to jelly as I roll slowly toward the flashing lights, my mind racing about all the possibilities I could be facing. I park two doors down, as close as I can maneuver. Getting out of the car, my pastoral adrenalin kicks in and I whisper a prayer for myself as I weave between a bright red rescue squad unit, its sister ambulance, then past an unmarked sedan with blue lights flashing from the deck and dashboard. I approach the porch where two EMTs stand solemn-faced. At the doorway, a stocky gentleman dressed in a brown rumpled suit steps out and extends his hand.

"Reverend, I'm Detective Richardson, with the Sheriff's Department. I'm glad you're here. Would you follow me, please?"

Richardson leads the way through the entry, through the living room, back to the kitchen, and then to the granite bar defining the den. He stops and motions me forward toward Molly, who is sitting on the sofa, surrounded on each side by women shielding her from intruders. Molly looks between them and spots me.

"Oh, Brother Boatwright, he's gone! He's dead!" She then bursts into tears as I pull up close to her, the women parting to allow me to sit to her right. I lean over, put my arm around her shaking shoulders and pull her close.

"I'm so, so sorry, Molly."

During the next half hour, I learn that Molly found Bill unresponsive when she went down to the basement to call him up for lunch. She called 911, and upon arrival, they determined Bill had no pulse, and wasn't breathing. The EMT's determined he had already passed, but could not declare the time of death. They notified the EMT medical director who had arrived about fifteen minutes later and declared Bill dead. Someone then notified the Sheriff's Office about an unaccompanied death, which required an immediate investigation, which in turn meant the coroner had to visit the scene. Meanwhile, the entire basement is cordoned off as a potential crime scene.

Molly has yet to notify her daughters, and is grateful her pastor is there to help her make the calls she dreads more than anything in the world. During those early moments of explanation, Molly's neighbors move silently into other rooms, fiddle around in the kitchen, staying within eyesight and earshot of their friend, but give her moments of privacy with her minister. It is during this privacy space that I quietly offer a prayer for Molly. When Molly's sister arrives, I rise, greet her, then step aside to honor their privacy and make my way to the back patio, where I find Officer Richardson smoking a cigarette.

"These are tough calls, aren't they preacher?" he mumbles through lips holding a lit smoke. He waits for my response.

"I'm shocked! I had just spoken to Molly by phone this morning, learned of Bill's loss of his job, and promised to drop by after lunch. I had no idea the situation was this critical. Can you tell me what happened?"

"At this point, not much to tell. We're waiting on the forensic team to examine the scene before we allow his body to be removed. Do you do last rites?"

"Not exactly, that's with the Catholics. But it might give some comfort to Molly and me if I offered a prayer in Bill's presence."

"Okay, I'll escort you down, but don't touch anything, or sit on anything. Just a precaution, no accusation."

Officer Richardson leads the way down to the outside entrance of the basement and enters ahead of me. I follow until we stand at the foot of the extended recliner. An ash-grey resemblance of a man I remember at his daughter's wedding is now stretched full length in silence, dull blue eyes staring at the ceiling.

With cautious motions of communication, watching for Richardson's approval, I lean forward and carefully place my hand on the cold, bare right foot. Holding it there gently, I quietly state: "Bill, I don't know what happened, but I know that you are a child of God, and you are in the presence of God's love. Peace, my brother."

I step back, turn and make my way out the sliding glass doorway. Richardson follows.

"What are your speculations at this point, Detective?"

"Tough to say. It has all the signs of a suicide, but so far we haven't found a note. As you can see, there was no evidence of violence. We'll have to wait for the autopsy report before we take any action one way or the other. Meanwhile, it's classified as a suspicious death."

"How long will the autopsy take?"

"Could be a while. We don't have the facility in this county. Have to take the case into Dekalb, and work it in between all the knife and gun cases from the weekend. Could be days, maybe a week or two, or more. Depends."

"As you might imagine, it would be very helpful for me to know as much as I can as I prepare his funeral." Handing Richardson my calling card, I continue, "I would appreciate any information you can give me."

"Same here, Reverend. Here is my card. We might be in touch."

I return to the family room, and over the next hour remain to support Molly, standing beside her as she calls each daughter and painfully relays the saddest of news. The forensic team comes and goes, followed by the mortician from the funeral home, Waynes and Waynes. They obtain basic information from Molly including Bill's name and other personal data, then respectfully remove Bill's remains from the home into the windowless van for transport to the coroner's office. They will be in touch to arrange a meeting at the funeral home at Molly's convenience. I promise to be available to Molly and leave her in the support of her neighbors. I take a slow drive back to my study at The Hill, and begin to process in my mind what I might say at the funeral.

⟵⟶

The next morning Reese Waynes calls me and explains that the family will be delaying the funeral for a few days. It will allow time for them to try to locate the other daughter and provide the time to make travel arrangements for everyone. Reese confirms that the family wants me to conduct the service, but they have not made up their mind whether to have the service in the church, at the funeral home, or just at the graveside. I respond with gratitude for the information and assure him that I will arrange my schedule and the availability of the church. My unexpressed interpretation for the delay is that it's a stalling tactic by the family, as they wait to see how the death will be ruled, thinking that if it was suicide, they might want to suffer their grief in privacy.

CHAPTER TWENTY-ONE

T uesday morning, I head toward the office earlier than usual to recoup from yesterday's re-direction and to get started on Bill's funeral. As I near the exit of our subdivision, I find myself stuck behind the Johnson County School District bus, red lights flashing, that requires me, the bus driver, and the commuters behind me to wait for a tardy, reluctant, un-groomed and obviously sleep-deprived second grader to plod her way down her long driveway and enter the bus. While I wait, I notice the big stone-walled entrance to our subdivision: Assisi Gardens.

I recall my trip with Marsha to Italy in 2010, our visit to Assisi, and the frescos in the Basilica of St. Francis, born Giovanni di Pietro. The relief on the curved concrete border of the intersection to my left depicts a wide collection of animals, wild mostly—a rabbit, squirrel, several species of fowl, large and small, a raccoon, a deer. Assisi Gardens is nestled in a pocket of the Georgia State Forest Preserve, marketed by its developer as an enclave where residents could observe wildlife from their kitchen window. The animal images embossed on the Assisi entry imply that the wildlife in this neighborhood is only of the genteel vein. Absent are bears, wolves, tigers—carnivores that might devour small children playing in the backyard.

With the child almost to the steps of the bus, my mind shifts from

St. Francis' love of animals to the same thirteenth-century saint's obsession with service to the poor—the call of the church to address its own opulence and to redirect its resources to the daily needs of humanity. As the bus pulls forward but continues to slow my progress toward that early start, my mind makes one more shift, deeper, recalling the conversion of Francesco Giovanni.

I try to piece together the story line from my memory. Though Francesco is the playboy of his day and the envy of his rich peers, he rejects his father's prosperous silk business. One day, he encounters a beggar in the marketplace. Francesco empties his pockets and gives the contents to the needy man. His father is outraged at this behavior. But after his personal theophany, Francesco unilaterally sells his father's inventory to help the poor. What follows is a confrontation between the merchant father and the penitent son, which ultimately causes the younger man to disown his family and take a vow of poverty. Today, we have his followers, the Franciscans—a worldwide religious order dedicated to care for the poor.

As the bus turns into the entrance of the elementary school, which clears a path to pick up my pace toward the office, I muse at the irony: half-million dollar homes nestled in a subdivision named after a saint dedicated to serving the poor! I also ponder the tensions evident in the Francesco tale—where business is viewed as the antithesis of righteousness, where one man's inventory contrasts with another man's sense of scarcity, where poverty seems to be correlated with purity and penance.

CHAPTER TWENTY-TWO

As Bill's funeral begins, my confidence in delivering words of comfort and hope to the family is much stronger than I had imagined possible when I left Molly the afternoon of Bill's sudden death. I took my usual approach to funeral preparation. I listened carefully while visiting family members in the intervening days. I spoke with new acquaintances during the visitation at the funeral home the evening before the funeral. I perused postings about Bill's awards on LinkedIn, Facebook, and newspaper archives. Bill was a highly respected forensic accountant, a term I had to Google to realize that he was a modern-day Sherlock Holmes who spent hours studying spreadsheets, financial statements, bank accounts, invoices, and cancelled check images. He gathered information that would either defend or accuse the target of the investigation, depending on which side was paying Bill to do the research.

Bill was a hired calculator who, over the course of his thirty-year career, had worked at various times for each of the nationally acclaimed big five accounting giants. I suspect that Bill's job put him in touch with the financial dirt on some of the highest-ranking people in business, making Bill the target of revenge from his then-current opponent. Little wonder that Bill was not considered to be a local socialite and life of the party. There was little he could say openly about those businesses and their leaders. Such was the inherent isolation of those who deal with facts that are extremely secret.

In the archives of the *Atlanta Journal* and the *Wall Street Journal* I discovered several reports where cases involving bribery, fraud, or insider trading and had been won or lost based on Bill's depositions. At the funeral home, Vicki, one of Bill's closest co-workers quietly related that Bill's superior expertise could be more of a burden than a blessing when seeking re-employment after being laid off. He knew too much about too many people for most potential employers to be comfortable with him in their ranks. He had worked himself out of the field. Vicki had talked with him three days before his death and learned that he had been turned down fifteen times for employment. The most common excuse was that Bill was overqualified for the job.

I also learned that Molly was mostly oblivious to what her late husband did in his profession. She knew he was an accountant, had always held a good job, and worked for large, prestigious firms. But she had no idea about the day-to-day details, which he understandably could not share over dinner or touching pillows.

In further digging, I also discovered that Molly worked at The Fabric Junction as an assistant store manager, in charge of stocking and maintaining the inventory of bolts of cloth. She also would measure and cut fabric for customers. Bill's income did not require her to work, but she picked up the low-stress job just to have something to do when the kids no longer needed her at home. She worked mostly for the discount available to her, as she was constantly revamping their modest home with the most current décor. Ten years Bill's junior, she held a degree in home economics but never desired to teach.

All this research gave me his professional credentials but little about him as a person. So with what I have, I do my best to carefully craft words of comfort and encouragement that acknowledge the reality of grief and offer support to family and friends.

Only in the weeks that follow the funeral do I begin to fully grasp some of the trauma associated with this death. In visits to the home, around the kitchen table, I coax Molly into conversations that reveal her deepest concerns, fears, and pain. Of immediate concern is how she will survive financially.

She believes Bill took care to provide adequate life insurance protection in the event of his absence. She estimates that he had more than two hundred thousand dollars of coverage on his life, partly from his group insurance with his employer, and partly from their personal policies to cover their obligations when the children were young and until they finished college. In fact, within the last two years, they had replaced some policies that were about to expire with new term life insurance coverage. The higher premium rates due to their age brackets had shocked them and required a more careful budgeting of their resources. Molly shares that what they thought was adequate coverage now might be in question. They had several policies—three, in fact—from different companies.

The company of the oldest policy, which amounted to only about fifty thousand, had taken the initiative to contact her within ten days following Bill's passing. They have promised a check for the full amount to be deposited directly into her checking account within a week. But the remaining policies are delaying their payment, pending the outcome of the investigation.

From my discussion with Molly and with my own insurance agent, Robert, I learned that life insurance policies typically have a contestability clause allowing postponement and potentially denial of benefit if the deceased dies within two years of purchasing the policy. If the insurance company proves that a health condition that led to the cause of death was not disclosed on the application, the beneficiary will only receive a refund of the premium that was paid. There is also provision of denial if the cause of death is determined to be suicide within the first two years of the policy. Furthermore, and perhaps more hurtful in Molly's case, if the coroner suspects that the death is a homicide and the beneficiary the prime suspect, all bets are off on getting a claim satisfied.

I fully expect the benefits to be delayed but not denied. Neither do I expect to be involved in any of these details except to support Molly—until I receive a call from Molly's sister, Jean. She calls to solicit my assistance, to intervene in the matter of Bill's estate. Jean wants me to step in and help stop the pilfering of her sister's estate by investment scam artists, including a few of their own relatives.

Do I dare?

CHAPTER TWENTY-THREE

Reggie makes his way past the row of well-worn booths at the Tic Toc and heads straight for the entrance to the back room. He is relieved to discover that he is not the first and therefore not the only participant in Pastor Jon's experiment. At the sideboard, he fills a thick, white porcelain cup with coffee, then pulls out a straight-back ladder chair to sit next to George.

"George, how are ya? Glad to see someone already here. Jon got you signed up for this, too?"

George grins. "Yeah, not sure what we got ourselves roped into. But Jon's been good to me and my family and I couldn't turn him down. Tough time to be here, though. This is cutting into my most productive time at the pharmacy."

"Tell me about it."

They sit in silence massaging their mugs, each in their thoughts about this breakfast with the pastor. Tom from the grocery and Virginia, a realtor, enter the room midstream of a mutual griping about the poor performance at the Falcon's game last evening. They grab coffee or tea and acknowledge George and Reggie as they find their seats across the table. The foursome banter about the failure of the de-fensive coach to put more emphasis on completing tackles. Reggie and George look at each other and, by their simultaneous glances at the Royal Crown clock on the back wall, silently communicate their concern that the host of this event has not yet arrived.

I can feel my blood pressure rising as I pull into the parking lot of the Tic Toc. As I grab my black leather folder and push past the chrome entrance doors, I ponder how children can choose the most critical mornings of my schedule to miss the bus. With my eyes set on the door to the back room, I do not take my usual inventory of those present in the dining room. I fear the back room will be empty. Or filled, but Roy will have forgotten to prepare the breakfast as promised. As I enter the room, the cacophony from the voices and the smell of fresh bacon, eggs, and grits dismiss my fears. I quickly greet each by name and thank them for coming.

My eyes meet Roy's from across the room, who signals that the food is ready to go, just waiting on the call to order.

"Lady and gentlemen, thank you for coming. I apologize for being late. Roy, thanks for preparing the food for us this morning. I know we all are pressed for time, so let's get down to it. Join me please in offering grace.

"We thank you, God, for all your blessings, for the privilege of sharing a meal together and a time of discussion. May you bless all that happens here this morning. Amen.

"Let's all grab some delicious eggs and bacon and as soon as everyone has served themselves and is seated, we'll begin our discussion."

I hold back from the quickly forming line and get a cup of coffee. I bring up the end of the line, with a piece of toast and slice of bacon on the plate as a gesture of sharing a meal, knowing I can't put anything in a stomach so unsettled. Within seconds of being seated, I begin.

"I again want to thank you for taking time out of your morning for this. To honor your very valuable time, I want to get right to it. As I have discussed with each of you, the purpose of these breakfast gatherings will be an opportunity for me to learn the issues that you face as owners or managers of your businesses. For some time now, I have been aware that much of what bothers you or stresses you is probably overlooked on my part. I would like to change that.

"I see this as an open forum, your forum, to share with me what is on your mind. Since this is our first gathering, such a dialogue might feel a bit strange and awkward. So, to sort of grease the wheels a bit, I have asked two of you in advance to share your thoughts this morning. Virginia is probably Verona's busiest realtor and Tom is our grocer and the owner of the IGA FoodFair. I approached these two to think about and to respond to two questions: 'What keeps me awake at night regarding my business?' and 'How does my business affect my personal life either positively or negatively?' Tom, would you share first?"

"Thank you, Pastor, I think. I'm not sure. I have to say this assignment was a bit of a challenge. I am not used to being asked this, particularly by a preacher. And I am not sure that I can freely share everything that has crossed my mind. Partly because I haven't thought some of it out completely, and partly because I am not used to revealing this type of information to others, not even my wife. So, I will try to honor your request the best I can, but maybe not fully.

"What keeps me awake at night? I would say one thing that falls in this category is when I have to let someone go. So much so that I sometimes delay terminating an employee and the situation only gets worse. Several things gnaw at me when it comes to making the decision to terminate someone. It is not so hard if they don't show up for work, or I find them stealing from me or lying to me. Those dismissals are tough, but rather clear-cut. It is bad for business to have anyone on payroll you cannot trust.

"No, the tough calls come when I have to let someone go because they are just not a right fit. Or the volume of business cannot support the current payroll and someone has to go. I've been there a few times myself, in my early years, when the kids were small and another on the way—being let go, I was told, not because I had done anything wrong, just that it was a business decision. Those were times in my own life when every paycheck was critical and jobs were scarce. I relive those moments in my mind when I make the decision to let someone go and again when I have to tell them. I'll tell you, Pastor, it is tough."

Several murmurs around the table tell me that Tom has struck a common chord among his colleagues.

"And that leads me to your second question: How does my business affect my personal life? My wife can tell when these types of decisions are laying heavy on me. She says I am grouchy, more so than my normal Oscar the Grouch demeanor, and she says I am hard to live with. In some cases, she knows the person I am going to have to let go, so I can't tell her—after all, it's a small town, you know.

"So, I would say, my business is in many ways my life. I live it, breathe it, ponder it, analyze it, like most of you here do, I am sure. So, Pastor, I hope I told you some of what you wanted to hear."

I allow just a few seconds of silence to let Tom's word sink in.

"Tom, thank you for sharing your thoughts. As you might imagine, my professional life as a pastor is just as closely interwoven into my personal life. It is hard to separate them. So, I hear that. However, I would have to say that I have very little experience in having to let someone go. There have been a few occasions where the church has had to make some tough decisions along these lines, but I seldom share the responsibility alone. Usually, a committee is involved and it becomes a long, drawn-out process. I would like to hear some more about issues like this, over the course of our gatherings.

"But right now I want to let Virginia speak. Virginia, what would you like to share with us about what keeps you awake at night and how your business affects your personal life?

"It's my clients who keep me awake at night. I don't mean they call me at all hours of the day and night, although sometimes they do. What I mean is that I find myself taking on some of their issues, their problems. I find myself getting involved way more than just trying to help them sell their house or buy another house. This is particularly true with my senior customers. Most of the time, they are selling their home because they must, not because they want to. It is a sad time for many of them, and I end up wanting to be the fix-it person, find them a happy solution.

"How does my business affect my personal life? I have no life! At least outside my business, anyway. It is probably good that I am single so I don't mess up some other person's life with all my weird hours and fretting over things I can't do anything about."

She blushes then continues.

"Now, guys, that is not a solicitation for a companion, so don't go trying to fix me up with someone. I'm okay being single.

"And I'm okay being in the business I'm in. Real estate fits me just fine. It is always feast or famine in this business, and right now I am in the rush of opportunities after many years of nothing moving. It is hard to keep up with everything. I need an assistant, but can't find the right fit yet. So, Pastor Jon, I'm not sure if that is helpful to you or not. But that's where I am."

"Thank you, Virginia. What you are sharing is actually very helpful."

I circle the room with my eyes. "I wonder if anyone else has anything to add."

In silence, everyone begins to look down at their coffee cups, and at the same time avoid eye contact with their peers.

"Preacher," Richard speaks from across the room, "I'm not sure what all this is about. I am grateful for the breakfast. I never could pass up a free meal. But I'm just not sure what you're wanting to get at here. I can agree with Tom, as probably most of you can, that laying off someone is one of the toughest parts of my job. I'd rather have a root canal—sorry, Andrew, to make such a comparison, and you did a fine job on me last week—but I'd rather do that than tell someone she's fired. So, what do you have to offer us this morning that can help this? Can you make this easier on us? Give us some better way to say 'you're fired'?"

There is a mixture of groans and chuckles in response to Richard's set-up. Then silence as everyone awaits my response.

I pause a moment further, then I look at him and speak calmly.

"Richard, I think you are on point to ask such a question. In fact, it's a question I'm asking myself as I hear your comments about letting people go. From everyone's reaction, I can see this is a common point of pain among most of you. Of course, I want to be the spiritual fix-it guy and offer you some immediate counsel on how to make these tough decisions better for you and for the individuals you have to let go.

"But of course, I can't. Not with any integrity. I cannot offer you a Scripture verse like a prescription to make it all better. But I can hear you. I *want* to hear you. Hopefully, that's what these gatherings will be about. I'd like to know what your concerns are, what the issues are, the tough issues that make up your lives. For some of you, business is your life. These tough areas probably get under your skin and into your heart and mind and affect the way you live. So, these gatherings may not give you a sense of immediate relief. But I am hoping they will help bridge communication between us. Between you and me, your pastor, and between each other.

"I am proposing to have these gatherings about twice a month— say, the second and fourth Monday mornings. We'll construct the sessions around three topics. The first will be feedback on one of the two sermons I would have delivered since our previous meeting. You can freely share your reaction to what I said. Maybe it is something positive, but it doesn't have to be. It could be something that bothered you, something that just didn't fit, in your opinion. You can offer any response you wish. Or you can just not say anything. I welcome any reaction at all.

"The second part of our gathering will focus on what I might preach about in the next two weeks. I will email you the Scripture passages I intend to address. I invite you to read them, ponder them a bit. Then I invite you to give me your feedback on the concerns and perhaps questions or challenges one or any of those passages bring to your mind. I will take your comments into consideration as I prepare those sermons. Again, you are not required to comment on them if you don't have anything to say, but you can freely speak your mind.

"The third part will be open and unplanned, allowing time for you to address any concerns you have individually or perhaps as a group. It would be an open agenda.

"What I promise you is that this will not be another Bible study or prayer breakfast. Of course, I am not saying there is anything wrong with those two forms of gatherings. They have their purpose and have served many of you very effectively in your spiritual development. No, this is something different. It is dialogue, a give and take, a chance to hear different perspectives. It is not so much to help you to change as it is to help *me* change. To help me understand and appreciate where you are, perhaps better understand where I am, or need to be.

"It is an experiment, really: a trial to see if something useful can come out of our getting together. I would like us to commit to this for a period of two months. That would mean we would meet four or five times. If we find it useful, we might continue. That would be up to you. But I ask you to give it at least this amount of time to see what might develop.

"I have talked with Roy, and he has graciously agreed to split the cost of these breakfasts with me. He and I are your hosts. You are our guests. We think strongly enough about the potential impact this gathering might have that we are willing to put forth the effort. Of course, in this case, it is Roy who has to get up early to bake the biscuits. But the point of this sponsorship is to make it as simple as possible and to remove any obstacles. We won't spend our time sorting out payment. We'll come, grab some coffee, have some good food, then let's talk, and then go about our workday. Twice a month.

"I'm not asking you to commit right now. Just think about it. We're scheduling another meeting for two weeks from today, same time. I've asked Bob, here, to help us go virtual to make it easy for everyone. Bob will send you an email to invite you to MeetUp.com. If you register, we can remind you of each meeting, and share the list of the Scriptures for the upcoming sermons. From the MeetUp notice, you can simply click and let us know whether you will attend or not. That way, Roy can know how many eggs to cook. If you don't want to share your email, we can work other ways for you to let us know if you want to participate in each meeting.

"So, that's it for now. Thanks for coming. If you have any questions, I'll stay around for a while or you can call me at the church for more information.

"Let me offer this as a blessing for our departure.

> *May the road rise up to meet you.*
> *May the wind always be at your back.*
> *May the sun shine warm upon your face.*
> *The rains fall soft upon your fields*
> *And until we meet again,*
> *May God hold you in the palm of His hand."*

CHAPTER TWENTY-FOUR

This afternoon, as I ponder the unfinished business of the morning breakfast meeting, Elizabeth buzzes me on the intercom. "Jon, Mr. Spike Cornelius is here to see you."

I am looking forward to this meeting, pre-arranged by a late-morning phone call. I go out to the reception area and welcome Spike into my study, where we each take a wing-back chair.

"Thanks for seeing me on such short notice, Pastor Jon. I just have a short break from the shop, so I'll get right to the point. I am disturbed about the situation between my brother and me.

"Yesterday, my preacher's sermon was about forgiveness, and it got me thinking. I probably need to do some myself in this situation. But I don't quite know how to do it, so I'm coming to you. I need to get some things off my chest, and I don't want to stir up new stuff with my pastor. He is new to the area and doesn't have the background about our family that you do. Since you already know some of the details—I emphasize *some*—I thought I would fill you in on more of the issues you might not be aware of since we last talked.

"Remember that I told you that in my early twenties, I left the business and the family. I was a hotshot then, thought I knew it all, and forced our old man to advance me my share of his estate. I did some things that embarrassed my family and embarrass me still today. Stop me if I seem to be repeating myself. And then I got saved, turned my life around, came home, and started back to work for Dad and my brother. I took the lowest position in the shop, cleaning the presses, packing and delivering the products, then moved up to maintenance of the shop. While I was at it, I went back to school and studied graphic design and production at the school where I had started and dropped out. I was able to finish my degree by using their online classes.

"You may not know that unbeknownst to Reggie and my father, I obtained field supervision for my practical work from a printing expert in Duluth who was also a graduate of Rochester. When I finished my bachelor's degree, he encouraged me to pursue a master's degree in business administration with a specialty in graphic production and manufacturing. He also supervised my capstone project. During this time, I continued to volunteer for extra assignments in the family shop. Reggie wasn't too keen on the idea, but from time to time, I would show Dad what I could do, and he would throw a few projects at me that seemed a bit off-the-wall to him. I was glad to get them and gave them my best shot. And most of the time, I succeeded. There were a few disasters, but he was forgiving. Dad began to recognize my contribution to the company, my insight into where the industry was going, and brought me up to management, put me in charge of marketing.

"At the time—this was in the late 1990s—printing was beginning to face a huge challenge, a lot of shops started to lose business, some of the smaller shops closing. There was a big shift to use computers for typesetting, graphic design, and layout. I volunteered to go to all the trade shows and soaked everything up I could learn about the future of the printing business, including digital printing and print-via-Internet. I convinced Dad just before he got sick to expand our business plan to accommodate a new print-on-demand press and the desktop publishing that went along with it. It was a steep layout of money. Reggie was opposed to making the investment, but Dad was favorable and won the day. I am glad to say that it was installed and online in time for Dad to watch its operation.

"He was blown away. Said it reminded him of when his printing experience went from linotype and letterpresses, to web presses, and then to offset presses. Unfortunately, Dad did not get to see the financial results of his investment. The recession hit around the same time we started the new division and a lot of our customers went out of business."

I urge him to continue, "So, what happened next?"

"Part of my administration degree focused on the multiple applications of graphic design and production, not just printing. It incorporated all the dimensions of visual media, including web design, brochures, print-on-demand books, branding—all the things we now take for granted in the industry. I spent a lot of time in Atlanta, visiting marketing agencies and telling them what we could do for them. In time, we won some very big contracts with companies like Sarah Lee, Claxton and Tom's. We even got a sub-contract for production of some NASCAR materials for their syndicated use. And it paid off. We are now the second-leading graphics production company between East Atlanta and Charlotte. We have captured more than twenty percent of the market share for what we do. And the Cornelius Printing Company is now a very profitable business. So much so, that I understand it is being pursued by Garnett Enterprises as an acquisition. I hear rumors, that the offer for our company is in the range of fifteen million, though Reggie won't share this with me."

I continue to listen but carefully avoid giving any confirmation or negation of data that I have learned in earlier discussions with Reggie. I signal that I am listening intently and expect Spike to continue.

"So, I suspect you know most of the details about the pending transaction. And that I am putting my nose into it. And that I am possibly gumming up the works by making some demands that I should be getting some of the proceeds of the sale, if it goes through.

"And I am quite sure Reggie has made you aware that he thinks I do not deserve any proceeds from the sale. He has told me in so many terms that I took my share long ago when he said I bailed on the family and left him and Dad to run the shop on their own. He's right, I have to give it to him, that whatever I took, I did some very foolish things with it. I blew it. I threw it away. Wasted it.

"But Pastor Jon, here is the point that seems to be overlooked. I helped make this business a profitable and therefore attractive purchase for some mega corporation. I don't want to bore you with the details of the industry, but here are some cold, hard facts that Reggie seems to be ignoring. The Internet market with eBay, Amazon, you name it, has taken a monstrous chunk out of commodity printing, the bulk of our business in the 1980s and 90s.

Spike moves forward to the edge of his chair, then continues.

"What I'm about to say may sound unkind. That's not the intent. I would sum up all this tension between Reggie and me this way: Reggie is old school when it comes to printing and he wants out. I'm new school. I'm what technology refers to as an early implementer. And when it comes to the printing business, I don't want to get out. I want to stay in, but do it differently.

"If it had not been for my leadership, pushing us to pursue business beyond putting ink on paper, we would be out of business. Our revenue growth has exceeded the national average by as much as double points for the last five years. We didn't attract a buyer because we are broke. We have someone who wants to buy us because we have survived the curve that spun away eighty percent of the printing businesses."

Spent, he relaxes back into the wingback and waits for my response.

"So, Spike, I hear your argument, but I'm not sure where I fit in. What can I do for you?"

"Pastor Jon, my minister emphasized yesterday that the Bible tells us that when your brother offends you, go to him and tell him, so you can be reconciled. I'd like to do that. My brother, Reggie, is offending me by shutting me out of the sale discussion, my future. He is also shutting me out of any consideration of having a share in our family estate. I'm aware of the will. I just happened to come across a copy of it and I know that I've been deliberately omitted. It was an old will, set up years ago, not long after I left on my hiatus. And it was never changed.

"The will declares that I made my choice and must live with it, that everything passes first to my mother and then to my brother at her death, including the assets the family owns, which also includes Cornelius Printing. That's the legal status. But it just isn't right. I've poured my heart and soul into this family business and I should be getting something in return. I ate my humble pie when I came back and started all over again in this business at the very bottom rung, working like a dog to pull myself back up the ladder. I felt my dad had completely forgiven me for making a fool of myself and my family. Felt Mom did, too. Felt they were proud of me. But it seems that is as far as it went—proud of me standing beside them in business, but not on paper."

I hear Spike's voice choke on this last point and witness a grown man holding back tears of anger and disappointment.

CHAPTER TWENTY-FIVE

T he following morning I look into my sleep-deprived red eyes as I whip the shaving soap. I cover my stubble with foam and review the possible source of my insomnia. What I remember is distressing, but not so much as to cause my eyes to repeatedly focus on the hairline crack in the plaster ceiling. In my sleep, I remember critiquing my performance of Bill's funeral, the search for clues in the faces around the breakfast table at the Tic Toc, the grass starting to grow faster than I can mow once very ten days—which reminds me of the vacation plans with the family. Would we visit parents again this summer? We need a break, just us, Amy and Rusty playing in the surf, I'm checked out, no agenda, no timelines outside of the tides.

I tap to flush the pepper specks from the razor and aim for the resistant cleft in my chin, thinking about the Oceana II just south of New Smyrna two years ago. A perfect vacation, worthy of repeating. I am glad Marsha booked the fourth week of June this year. Expensive, almost $2,000 for the seven days, but worth every penny. Which reminds me what has also prevented my sleep—taxes. The sequence is spring, tax returns, tax refund, vacation funding, vacation time, in that order. It is April 12 and I have not scheduled my annual appointment with my accountant, Toller Cooper, nor have I even started gathering all the documents to support my expenses, housing allowance, and mileage.

On my way to the office, I call Cooper Tax Services and apologetically beg my way into an appointment tomorrow morning.

⌁

"Toller, thanks for seeing me and working me in. I know you're slammed right now and I know you shouldn't even consider seeing me at this late date. I am really sorry."

"No problem, Jon. I have come to anticipate your timing and reserved a slot for you this week. Coffee? Tea?"

For the next twenty minutes, Toller sifts through the contents of a well-worn legal file pocket, asking me questions about the sofa and end tables we bought in August, honorariums for funerals and weddings, and the mortgage statement. When his questions on tax documents seem satisfied, he re-packs the papers into the pocket and comments without direct eye contact, "The word on the street, Jon, is that you're starting to get some traction with the local business folks. How's that going?"

"Well, we've just started, really. We'll see. Why don't you join us?"

"Impossible this time of year. Maybe in May, if you're still holding court."

"Toller, I'm glad you brought up these breakfast meetings. I'll look forward to having you in the group. I think you'll add some interesting perspective to our discussions. However, I've got an issue right now that I need some advice on from you. Can I buy you lunch?"

"Lunch? This week? No way. Sorry, Pastor. But check with me in ten days. Unless you need to alert me to someone about to commit suicide over some tax fraud, it will have to wait. In the next seventy-two hours, the only thing I will be doing other than filling out tax forms at this desk is taking two-hour naps. And then, April 16th, I'm going off to my cabin on the lake to chill for four days. No phone, no clock, no family, no nothing. I'll be in a better mood to hear you after that. Let's do lunch on Tuesday, May 5th, at Tolteco's.

"Debbie will have your taxes ready at the front desk tomorrow morning. Just sign them, you and Marsha, and drop them back by here. We'll file them electronically and hopefully, you"ll be set for funding your vacation."

We rapidly take turns dipping tortilla chips into the salsa, as I ask, "Did you have a good tax season, Toller?"

"Biggest year yet. I do love our government. The more complicated they can make our tax code, the more confidence I have in funding my retirement."

"Thanks for doing ours again this year. I don't really expect you to do my taxes *gratis* every year. I am grateful for the zero billing, but more importantly your guidance on the strategies. I'd be lost without you. "

We tap our margarita salt rims. *"Cinco de Mayo,"* we say in unison.

"Toller, I want your view on an issue that is starting to stress me. I am struggling with just how much I should be involved in people's finances, their businesses."

"Go on."

"I have a situation—you are probably aware of it, but I cannot disclose the details—where a relative of someone whose husband has died has asked me to help protect his wife from being fleeced. Do you ever have any of that come up in your business?"

"Matter of fact, too much. You would not believe what I hear about the squabbles that are going on between siblings and spouses. And don't get me started on all the trash I learn about people going through divorce. Truth is MUCH stranger than fiction, in my line of work. I'm a numbers guy. Throw numbers, tax codes and account rules at me all day and I'm in my element. But people tell me the strangest things that are completely out of my league."

"Tell me more."

"For example—and I have to be discreet here, so I'll use a case many years back—two sisters get into a battle over the settlement of their grandfather's property. They are the only heirs remaining. One is the executor, and the other accuses the first of fraud and misappropriation of funds used to fix up the old family property that no one in the family wants. I happen to have both of them as tax clients, and each of them spill out all kinds of stories about the other while I sift through taxable receipts and W-4s. One is suing the other, has retained a lawyer, and all over a $3,000 bill to paint the house, so it can be put up for sale. And they both go to my church. Won't even speak to each other. I'm a deacon, in fact assigned to both of them. I've tried to get them to calm it down, but no luck.

"Now that you are asking me," Toller continues, "this kind of thing is out of my field, but each sister, independently, has ranted in my office about the perceived injustice of the other. This is an example of where my pastor should be able to step into the middle of this and help them sort out this family mess that is dividing the family and even dividing the church. We cannot even get through a nominating committee agenda without this strife between these two sisters being a part of our decision-making. Unreal. But the pastor—my pastor—is hands-off. Won't touch it. Like it doesn't exist. And we, the congregation, sitting in the pews, wonder why.

"Preacher Jon, you asked, and I'll tell you. I think your profession—maybe not you, but your kind—is ducking the tough stuff of families and individuals. So, let me be frank here. I think you're headed in the right direction, with your increased interest in the business part of our lives, but you are just scratching the surface. I wish you and your colleagues would step up to the plate and get in the game, so to speak."

"Tell me more, Toller."

"Okay, since you asked. There is a family, a friend of a friend, in South Georgia, who grew up on a farm raising pecans, peaches, and peanuts—the three 'Ps.' He has three siblings, all of whom have made good careers. One brother has hit it big-time in Silicon Valley as an IT start-up specialist. One sister finished her dental schooling and is making a good living with her husband and three kids in Charlotte. And the other brother, the youngest, is having the time of his life traveling all over the world as a pilot for Delta Airlines.

"Meanwhile, my friend, Oscar, the oldest brother, has stayed with the homestead, keeping up the farm, working with the parents. The father of this clan had a stroke last year. I believe he is in his late eighties, worked up until he collapsed in the orchards. He can no longer work the farm. And the mother is showing signs of dementia, maybe early Alzheimer's. Meanwhile, a mega national agriculture conglomerate is chomping at the bit to buy the 700-acre estate. They want to take it over and run it like a corporation instead of a family farm. It is obvious that the old folks can't stay on the homestead much longer. The family—and particularly my friend, Oscar—are feeling the pressure to sell. I've heard that the offer is three million cash.

"Now, here is the sticky part. The company making the offer wants to buy the whole thing—the orchards, the fields, and the homestead. Knock down the barns, put in irrigation systems, replace the homestead with a small operations office, leaving my fraternity brother Oscar with no place in the new arrangement, including nowhere to live. They plan to bulldoze the home. What's he to do? He is too old to start over. He is in his fifties with an agriculture diploma from Abraham Baldwin Community College."

"That's a tough situation, Toller. What's going to happen? How do you see this fitting in with a pastor's job?"

"In my opinion, Pastor Jon, the person who has the most to give and to lose on this matter is the family's pastor."

"Go on, what has the pastor got to lose?"

"More about that in a moment. You'll see.

"What I think should happen is that the pastor should call for a kitchen table meeting with all the members of the family and talk about this problem."

"What do you mean, 'talk about it'?"

"I mean that there are some expectations building in those family members that are going to blow the family apart if everyone tries to get his own way. There is a family fight just brewing under the surface. Here is how that goes…

"The family knows outright that AgraCon has made an offer for the farm and everything, for three million. The children and the parents also know two other facts: a) AgraCon will come in and knock down everything, including the farmhouse, requiring the parents to leave, and b) the parents' health conditions do not look good. In fact, they are not expected to live more than a year. As I see it, there are several estate settlements in the works. Each member of the family is thinking about how this estate is going to shake out and what they are going to get out of it. In some cases, they have even over-mortgaged each of their homes and done nothing for retirement, expecting this estate to be their golden ticket to bail them out.

"In a nutshell, pardon the pun, here is what I think should happen. The pastor calls a meeting of the family on behalf of the parents, by their request or with their permission. Maybe it's in the kitchen of the family farmhouse, the Saturday after Thanksgiving. The pastor might explain that the parents are reaching the end of their lives and want to make sure their children are in good relationship with each other when they die. The parents would like to end their days knowing that the estate to be divided up is settled and agreed to by all concerned.

"The pastor takes a third-party position and offers this observation:

Three of the siblings have had the opportunity to go off and establish very good careers that seem quite fulfilling and profitable, of which their parents are genuinely proud. However, the oldest son, Oscar has stayed close to home, taking care of the parents, first by assisting with them with running the farm, and finally taking over the farm for them. His presence close to home has allowed the parents to live their lives in comfort and care. At the end of the day, his income has not been anywhere near the category of his siblings in their professional careers.

"The pastor goes on to share common knowledge: the farm is up for sale, and will probably be sold in the next six months. Conventional wisdom holds that the expected division of the parents' estate is to be equal: the selling price of the property is divided equally among the siblings. Equal seems, in most cases, to be fair. But equal in this case might not be fair. When the farm sells, Oscar the son will lose his place of residence, because the farmhouse will be razed. While Oscar the son has worked this farm along with his parents, he has had a meager income—enough to get by, mind you, but there has been no 401K or IRA arrangement for his retirement. So, if he gets one-fourth of the estate, he is starting from zero with that amount while his siblings are adding to their already-established incomes and retirement plans. His siblings were able to earn those high incomes, and to put aside retirement funds, without having to worry about Mom and Dad, because Oscar was taking care of them all these years.

"The pastor explains that to divide their parents' estate in fourths might seem equal, but is it fair? What the parents might want their children to understand and accept, is that the division of their estate should be fair rather than equal. And they want their children's blessing on this.

"Then comes the time for the pastor to wait for their responses, to listen, and to guide them through an honest discussion about their reaction to this request by their parents."

"So, Toller, why do you think this is the pastor's role? Shouldn't this be a discussion conducted by the estate attorney or someone like yourself, the family CPA?"

"The attorney is there to protect the wishes of the parents and to construct the legal language that will provide that protection. The CPA, myself included, is the numbers and tax professional. We, at least I speak for myself, are not comfortable getting into the family weeds in conversations like this. Give me numbers, give me spreadsheets with columns and dates and values, and I can give you my best professional service. But I know very little about family issues. Hell, I can't even understand my own family at times.

"In my opinion, it is the minister's pastoral training that helps sort out stuff beyond the legal and accounting. You can have the best legal document and the best financial data and it can all fall apart if there is no trust. In fact, I read just the other day that seventy percent of estate plans fail. And the number one reason given by those who watched their estates evaporate wasn't incompetent legal advice, wasn't poor management of investments. The number one reason for failures is the lack of trust between the family members and the trustees. A lack of communication, suspicion, assumptions—you name it.

"So, Toller, what happened in your friend's situation, this farm buyout by AgraCon?"

"They never had that conversation around the kitchen table. The property sold for four million. The parents died within months of each other three years ago. The estate settlement is still tied up in the courts. I'll have to give their pastor some credit, though. He showed up at the nursing home as regular as clockwork, offered prayers for the mother, who was out of it until she died. And he spent a lot of time with the father in his final days and was there with the family for many hours in the hospital room or waiting room. And he conducted two beautiful funerals. But he never once, as my friend shared with me, discussed with the parents or the siblings the storm that was brewing for over two years before the parents died."

"And Toller, why do you suppose he didn't?"

"Not sure I can answer that. Maybe you can. Why do you think he avoided that discussion?"

"My guess? He was afraid he might lose his job."

CHAPTER TWENTY-SIX

Molly greets me at her back door and ushers me into her kitchen to a seat at the table which just a few months ago was loaded with cakes, pies, casseroles, and gallon jugs of sweet tea. That feast was the response of a community who responded to the news of her husband's sudden heart attack. Today, that table is covered by a well-worn red plaid vinyl tablecloth and a single placemat. Molly offers me a cup of coffee. She remembers that, like Bill, I prefer my coffee strong and black.

In the first weeks following Bill's death, I frequently sat at this table to help move the Squires family through the many facets and stages of grief. Their kids had also crowded around this table to discuss the details of the funeral service.

I had planned to come by later in the week to check on Molly's progress, but she called and asked me to come today. Taking a bite of a slice of fresh pound cake, I begin the conversation.

"Molly, how are the kids and grandkids? Adjusting now that the routine of school is well underway?"

"The three grandkids are as active as ever. The oldest, Trey, is now 16 and able to drive on his own. He drops by frequently to check on me and mow my lawn."

She continues the conversation in another direction.

"Pastor Jon, yesterday I had a visit from the Academy Life Insurance Company, an agent, a Mr. Knowles presented me with this." She slides a check-size piece of paper across the red plaid toward me.

"I need to talk about this," she says nervously, then adds, "Never imagined I would be faced with this much money." I flip over the check and see it is from the Academy Life Insurance and Annuity Company of Nebraska, made payable to Molly Leslie Squires, Beneficiary for Bill Lewis Squires, in the amount of $75,000.00.

I am quickly relieved that Bill took some good action long ago to help his beloved wife survive his absence. My eyes linger over the check and I realize before I speak that I have misread the amount. It is not for $75,000.00. I am not familiar with this many zeroes. It is for $750,000.00. *Holy Jesus, this is three quarters of a million dollars.*

Before I can gather my thoughts, Molly pushes an opened envelope over to me and says, "This also came in the mail this morning."

I glance up at Molly and sees her brown eyes are welling with tears. I pull open the envelope and read a letter from Henderson Forensics, Inc., Steubenville, Ohio.

…we are deeply grieved at the loss of our beloved employee Bill and will forever remember his work ethic as a model for other employees.

It is hand-signed by the president of Henderson Forensics, Inc. Sliding from the folds of the letter is another check, this time from Madison Employee Benefits and Insurance, Beallsville, Kentucky, made payable to Mrs. Molly. L. Squires. This time, I carefully study the payable amount. My lips read, "Two hundred fifty thousand dollars." I notice the memo line reads, 'Employee Death Benefit for Bill L. Squires.' I mentally add and realize I am sitting at the table of a millionaire, a sudden and shocked millionaire, wrapped in grief, with no experience with large finances.

I pause for a moment to take in this scene and ponder my role. When my eyes again meet Molly's, I am aware that I could be venturing into financial territory that is well beyond my pay grade. But I am also smack in the middle of what it means to deliver pastoral care. I take another bite of pound cake, then another sip of coffee, buying time to think of how I will respond. Nothing I can recall in my seminary classes in pastoral care or church administration comes readily to mind. As the coffee clears my throat, I ponder for a second if I should take another bite of pound cake.

Falling back on my natural pastoral skills, I reply, "Molly, I sense you are completely surprised by these two events. Is that correct?"

"Oh, Pastor Jon, I am in complete shock! Bill and I would talk occasionally about our finances. We always were careful about our debt. I trusted him to pay the bills and we always talked before we made any kind of purchase like a car or something. He was never one to talk about death, or one of us having to live without the other. He always said I would be taken care of and I just trusted that. I did not know how it would come about, but figured he had everything planned out.

"We had been planning on retirement, having everything paid off when we reached the maximum age for Social Security for each of us. We only had three more years to go on our thirty-year mortgage on this house. He just put a new roof on it last year. The cars are paid for. He wanted to retire this year but decided we needed him to work seven more years until we were both eligible for Medicare. Since he passed, I have been concerned about how to pay for healthcare coverage for the next eight years."

Molly's gaze drifts somewhere through the kitchen window to a spot on the back lawn as her voice goes soft and then quiet.

"Molly, Bill might not have talked much about taking care of you, but he took some serious actions some time ago to make these resources available to you now. What are some of your thoughts now that you have received these checks?"

"My thoughts are all over the place. Since that delivery yesterday, my stomach has been in a knot. Sounds crazy, doesn't it? One day, I am worrying about how to buy health insurance until I get Medicare and the next, I have all this!

"I didn't sleep a wink all night. A thousands things were rolling around in my head. I thought I was settling down and starting to move toward a normal routine the best I can. I am glad my oldest son took care of the funeral details and the cost of the service and burial. Thank you again for the wonderful job you did. The gravestone arrived last week and it looks wonderful. Hard to see it, but it helped put a closure to part of it."

I realize she has avoided answering my question. Is she just naturally rambling, or is she uncertain of how to answer? I continue to listen.

"My stone is right next to his, with my date to be added."

She pauses for a moment and I see that she is preparing to go on, perhaps into some deeper thoughts that she wants to share, so I wait.

"After about a week, the regular bills started coming in. I didn't know what to do. I had my own checkbook, but he took care of all the monthly bills. I had a tax bill from the county. Stuff just kept coming, and I felt I was drowning. A friend of mine recommended Joy Gilstrap. She helps widows like me organize all the bills and mail and paper stuff that just overwhelmed us. She came over immediately and worked miracles. Helped me get up to speed on who to pay and when. I couldn't have managed through it without someone like Joy. Bill always did our taxes because he liked the challenge, even though he groused for a month getting all the stuff together and filing it. Joy put me in touch with an enrolled agent, James, who quickly took that burden off my mind.

"Pastor, you would think with two checks like these I would be dancing, figuring out where I could travel. Maybe throwing a big party. A part of me wants to do that. But the other part started thinking about all the things around me. Should I pay off the mortgage?

We had enough in savings that I could use to do that, but I would have had very little in reserve.

"Someone recommended Bobby, an estate attorney, who helped me begin probating the will. Glad we had that. But now I don't know how that fits into all this insurance money. I find it very lonely here at night, so my sister suggested having her 18-year-old daughter come live with me while she attends the community college here. But she has a boyfriend who looks to be no-good to me, and he is always hanging around."

Molly's thoughts spill out like windblown tumbleweeds, disconnected, random. I let each spin out its energy before being bumped by the next.

"Pastor Jon, what do you think I should do? I want to do the right thing."

Before I can respond, another tumbleweed spills out.

"I never dreamed I would have this much money. I've had my silly dreams about what I would do if I won the lottery. Give a lot of it away, make my friends and family happy with gifts I have always wanted to give. Travel around the world. Give the church a big gift. Drive a new car every year. But this is different.

"Last night, I could think of thousands of ways to use this money. My oldest boy, Ricky, is okay. He earns a good living, but I could help him with Trey's college. Maybe he would go to college if someone paid his way. And my other son, you remember Leslie, he's out of work, has been for over a year. His wife needs a hysterectomy, and they don't have any health insurance. They are about to lose their house. Speaking of houses, earlier this week I had the third offer to buy this one. Some folks are telling me to sell this place and move on. I am not so sure, but I do know it is hard to keep up this yard. We had trouble with the oil heater last winter and I might have to replace it.

"Pastor Jon, you know very little about me, mostly because I keep everything to myself. I am a very private person. But I don't know where to turn."

A lengthy pause clues me that Molly is now ready for a response. For the moment, she is empty, but only for the moment.

I place a hand on the checks and, looking up, I gently speak.

"Molly, Bill took great care of you after he could no longer be with you. Long ago, he did all of this with you in mind. You were primary in his thoughts. I understand your sense of shock. And I also appreciate your sense of being overwhelmed. There are indeed a lot of things to work through. They will require careful thought in order to make the best decisions for you. This unexpected resource in a time of grief seems a source of blessing for you."

I pause to make sure she is taking this in. She just fiddles with the hem of the tablecloth.

"I sense there are several things going on in you at this moment. One is to discover how best to use these new resources in a way that will help you, not just today and next week, but for the rest of your life.

"The other thing at work here is the practice of your faith in a setting that is unfamiliar to you. You might say, by most standards, you are now a very wealthy lady. And now you have new resources you must manage. I believe that your faith will guide you to make the best decisions for yourself as Bill intended. I will be at your side to help you through those times, and you can call on me anytime you want to discuss such matters."

"Pastor, I wouldn't have the first clue of where to turn. That's part of the reason I called you today. I know your expertise is not financial stuff, but all of this money has suddenly made me a bit uncomfortable. I don't know what to do, but I want to do what is right. What do you suggest?"

"You're right, Molly. My strongest suits are teaching and preaching.

But you're also right in that events like today are some of the very areas where our faith is explored beyond our usual comfort zone. I want to work with you on this.

"As your pastor, I am deeply concerned about your welfare. I have seen many cases where relatives, friends, even strangers come out of the woodwork in attempts to get their hands on someone's good fortune. I don't want that to happen to you. So, I am suggesting you take a few simple steps to get some professional help in two areas.

"I suggest you not cash these checks until after you have spoken with an attorney who specializes in estate planning. I can help you find one if you need me to.

"Second, I recommend you find a good financial advisor. You might want to shop around for one who suits you. I know a few, and I will be glad to provide you with their contact information.

I pause and let Molly absorb these suggestions. As she picks up the conversation again, I sense that she is much less tense and is beginning to discuss more of her concerns in an orderly fashion much as she has always done, even in the early stages of her grief. A few minutes later, after another cup of coffee and another slice of pound cake, I send all the usual signals that I must leave for other appointments. I offer to pray with a question.

"Molly, we have addressed some very important and new things in your life today. As we pray, is there anything specific you would like me to include for you?"

She mentions a desire for a sense of peace, guidance, and healing.

I offer a simple prayer of gratitude for Bill's kindness and thoughtfulness many years ago and for the ongoing grace of God that sustains and guides us in times of grief, in times of need, and in times of blessings.

CHAPTER TWENTY-SEVEN

As I leave my house for the fourth business group breakfast, I am feeling confident this discussion model is producing results. After only three meetings, I sense an openness and comfort. I am also gaining traction with the business people through our honest discussions. They are not letting me off the hook. By the third session, it was a no-holds-barred atmosphere, though the dialogue remained civil.

This morning, I am eager to hear their reaction to my sermon last week about the Gospel that relates the story of equal pay for workers who labored for varying parts of the day. But I am more excited about their questions about a future Scripture reading—the one about King David arranging the death of his military chief of staff so he can claim his wife as his own.

As I enter the back room, there is a sense of excitement. We have grown by four additional business people and the room is starting to get just a bit crowded. Everyone seems to be glad to be present, and the chatter is lively about everything from government interference affecting business profit to the latest standings in professional baseball. I offer the opening prayer for our meal and we all dive into the breakfast that might make our personal physicians cringe.

I finish my meal and remain seated as usual, but call the group to order.

"Ladies and gentlemen, thanks again for coming and for your participation. I'm gaining a great deal from these sessions, and I hope you're enjoying them, as well."

The sounds of approval are various, from forks clinking drinking glasses to scattered applause. I am feeling the glow.

"So, as we have done previously, we will open the floor for feedback and discussion on the sermons delivered in the past two Sundays. Who wants to go first?

"I recognize Andy, from the Savings and Loan. What say you, Andy?"

"Well, Pastor, I just want to say thank you for this forum. I really look forward to it each time. I had planned to yield my time to a colleague who has something special he wants to say, but I look around and he is not here yet. Oh, there he is, Reggie Cornelius."

Reggie walks in from the kitchen entrance and, with a bit of a grin on his face, stands at the head of the long table and opens his mouth to speak.

"Brothers and sisters, I just want to say how much I appreciate what brother Jon is offering in these sessions."

Reggie's voice sounds unlike him. High-pitched, squeaky, shrill.

A few guys start to giggle.

"As you all know, Brother Jon conducted my mother's funeral. I thought he did such a wonderful job, and I requested a copy of the eulogy he so eloquently delivered on that occasion. I thought I would share a few lines with you."

More adolescent giggling from these adults, some starting to snicker.

Reggie reaches into his jacket pocket and pulls out several sheets of paper that look like my sermon manuscript. He begins to read:

"As we are all aware, Miss Martha Grace Cornelius was one who was known for neutering all those around her. When it came to her husband in his illness, she neutered him. And her two sons benefited from her neutering from their earliest years and even into adulthood."

Bill, at the end of his table, spews coffee from uncontained laughter. Virginia squeals. Roger knocks over his juice glass, grabbing his napkin to cover his mouth. I am stunned, not knowing what is happening, and embarrassed at the jab at my carefully crafted sermon that now has words I do not recognize. *Neutering?*

Reggie is laughing so hard he cannot contain himself, the script falling from his hands as he slaps his knees and lets out the squeaky, high-pitched laughter that sounds like a cartoon chipmunk.

I reach down, pick up the manuscript and search it frantically for the clue to this riot at my expense. There it is. Highlighted in yellow. "Neutering," "Neutering," "Neutering," "'Martha Grace was a neutering member of The Hill."

I feel my face flush red and hot.

All eyes turn to me, some wet from laughing so hard.

"Brother Jon, it appears you hit the wrong key on your spell check. I checked with my doctor and he said that indeed I have not been neutered, but the effects of this helium should wear off by the time you get back to your office and correct the spelling in this eulogy. I look forward to a corrected copy I can give my grandchildren."

Now I am laughing, embarrassed, but laughing at myself. It is obvious that this group cannot go forward today with any serious discussion, so I just leave the agenda wide open. And it turns out to be our best gathering yet.

CHAPTER TWENTY-EIGHT

I stand politely with briefcase in hand as the receptionist dials three numbers and says, "Dr. Dan, Rev. Boatwright is here to see you." She motions to me with her eyes that I can enter the office behind her.

Dr. Dan is still bowed over papers in the center of his desk, the desk light reflects off his bald spot. To each side of whatever Dr. Dan is reading are three irregularly stacked towers of bound presentations, some with plain white bond paper and others bound in distinctly colored covers.

"Good to see you, Jon," Dr. Dan says without looking up from the page he is marking with a fountain pen filled with blood-red ink. He motions with his free hand for me to take one of the two seats facing each other next to the window. "Be right with you."

I sit in silence, gazing out at the campus, admiring the massive pin oak that shades the window and the sprawling lawn two floors below. After a snap of the fountain pen cap and the squeak of his swivel chair, Dr. Dan takes the chair next to me.

"Really good to see you," he repeats. "I've read your proposal and I like where you're headed. It seems to me that you have acquired ample material with real-life experience, Scripture, and other materials. Looks like you are set to dive in to this matter of intersecting faith, business and economics. How do you feel about it?"

I exhale, uncross my legs, and ease the briefcase to the floor. I realize I don't need to defend the efforts of my proposal. I finally have an ally, and it is time to claim the support he is offering me.

"Dr. Dan, I guess you are hitting the target squarely—asking how I feel. I sense that you are approving my project?"

I cannot hide my grin as he reciprocates.

"But I confess I am experiencing some angst about how to wrap it up. I've got good, honest dialogue going in my breakfast meetings with business leaders. I am finding good reception to my sermons that now have some connection, where appropriate, with the world of business. So, I am excited about where this is taking me. I am learning a lot."

I collect my thoughts and determine if I have the courage to move deeper. I sip the latte I brought with me, as I hope that Dr. Dan will pick up the conversation, which doesn't happen. I sense his eyes are looking directly into my soul so I disrupt the eye contact by carefully watching how I place my paper coffee cup on the corner of a side table covered in randomly stacked books. Dr. Dan waits.

"I underscore that I am learning a lot. I hope my parishioners are, as well. They seem to be. However, I am a bit anxious about how to tie all this up neatly in my final project presentation."

"Tell me more."

"Well, it seems to me that after six months of concentrating, of paying attention to the way economics and business and faith intersect, I'm just scratching the surface. I fear two things: One, that I will not be able to close this project neatly with definitive conclusions—empirical evidence that my efforts are making a difference. I fear I will get shot down upon trying to defend my project with statistics—or I should say, the lack of statistics. Much of what I can report will be anecdotal, subjective."

"And? You mentioned two fears."

"The second fear is that I cannot see a neat closure to all of this. Some of my colleagues have projects that have a clear beginning and end. Like Dave Millen, for example, who has a summer project that applies several ministry concepts to the housing project near his church. Or Rachelle, whose project is on Advent as a metaphor for new life in her dying church. I just don't see a nice, tied-up ending to what I'm doing. The whole idea of business and faith just continues to unravel in a multitude of ways. I feel like I'm starting to chase rabbits that don't exist, or if they do exist, they seem unending, unresolvable."

I take another sip of coffee, hoping Dr. Dan will pick up the conversation, but it does not occur. He remains focused on my eyes.

"I guess the real fear is that I will start to drown in this subject matter; that I will overdo it. I have to check myself that I don't try to see a business transaction in every verse of Scripture. I'm afraid my congregation will get sick of hearing about business; that people who have no connection with business will turn away."

I scoot a bit down into my chair and lean back, and place my arms on the side rests. I try to signal that my academic belly is exposed, that the ball is now in my professor's hands. I wait. He seems to be taking in all that I confessed and is getting ready to reply.

"Jon, those are legitimate fears. I say they are legitimate to acknowledge that they are real to you. But they may not be bad. From where I sit, I think those fears could be cautioning you on how you're going to move forward. Let's talk first about your last fear. What I hear is a fear of oversaturation in connecting business and faith. Is that a good way to describe what you are saying?"

"Exactly. What I couldn't or wouldn't see before, I'm seeing everywhere."

"Jon, what you're experiencing is common. It happens in every venue of life. When I first met my wife, Samantha, I had never really paid attention to redheads. I've been happily married to her for thirty-seven years and I swear every redhead I see makes me pause, turns my head if only a degree. We spent months calculating what car we would buy next. I looked and looked, convincing myself that I would not follow fads and buy what everyone else was buying. I wanted it to be a smart decision, not an impulsive, emotional reaction orchestrated by a salesperson on the showroom floor. We studied and shopped, and finally made our purchase on what I thought was a rare selection. But now, driving down the freeway, or into Midtown, I see my car being driven by others all the time. I never knew there were so many fans of Nissan Jukes. I thought they were too ugly to be popular, but apparently there are a lot more folks who are as fond of ugly as I am.

"My point is this. Once you have been sensitized to seeing things another way, from another perspective, you see evidence of those differences all around you. My wife is a photographer. She pays close attention to colors—natural colors, outdoor colors. She knows the difference between morning light, high noon, afternoon and dusk. She even sees blue in a midnight sky. I never knew such colors or shades existed before I met her. Now, I see blues, different shades of blue in a sunset that take my breath away.

"Now, you bring up a good point in that not everyone will appreciate or even see what you see. And if you go overboard on some area of fascination, it can be a real turn-off or even a put-down to others. But that is not to say you should abandon what you are learning to see. It just means you have much to learn, more to learn, about what else is out there to see as never before.

"So, probably the biggest takeaway from this project is that you are documenting your journey of how you process this new way of looking at faith and business. How will you continue to learn? How will you continue to apply what you learn? How far do you push what you learn with others? What is the right time to apply what seem to be new approaches? You are getting in touch with the same thing your predecessors over the ages have experienced. You are processing life and civilization."

"Jon, you are onto the real purpose for this doctoral degree—becoming a lifelong student, a reflective practitioner. You are getting into the realms of our lives that can be overlooked but have profound implications on how we find solutions to our problems. So, I'd have to say 'hooray' for your fear. It's a good thing."

Now he pauses, but not long enough for me to initiate a thoughtful reply.

"My challenge to you is to explore how you are going to process in your life and your ministry these ongoing opportunities for growing. Not just your growth, but the growth of those you want to serve. How do you balance your curiosity with the lack of it in other areas of your life? How do you deal with your own curiosity when you are surrounded with people who seem to have none?

"Which leads me to your other fear. What I hear is a fear that you will not be able to wrap up this project in a nice, little tight bundle that says, 'I studied this, I did this, and this is the result of what I studied and what I did.' That is nice for academia. It makes a nice whitepaper presentation. But it seldom represents life and rarely demonstrates true ministry.

"One of the faults of the Doctor of Ministry approach is how it sometimes tries to force conclusions prematurely. By that, I mean the time limitations can place artificial boundaries on what is actually happening to the student and where the student applies his research. I have seen enough of these projects over the past twenty years to know that some were packaged and presented when they were too green. The evidence, the results, were premature.

"So, to your fear of trying to wrap up your project. That fear is probably a reality that we cannot easily ignore, given that you have to make a formal presentation and defense of your work in the next several months. But what I would like to challenge you to do is to take your project wherever it leads you and let that be the project. It might be that all your study leads you to is a precipice of uncertainty, the scariest of places in the application of faith and ministry. But that might be just what you need to say, what you have learned, and what you will continue to learn."

I sit across from my consultant, taking a moment to absorb what I have just heard, before responding.

"I have to admit that is not what I expected to hear from you this morning. You are asking me—or giving me permission, I'm not sure which—to stick my neck out on this degree. Do I have your backing if I do?"

"Frankly, I would find it delightful. However, I cannot guarantee your protection. Review committees have their own autonomy when it comes to signing off on awarding doctoral degrees. But I will be by your side, defending your right to explore with integrity where your study will have taken you and where it might open your horizons for future growth."

CHAPTER TWENTY-NINE
SPIKE

The two phone lines blinking above Trish's active line are increasing the typical mid-morning stress—calls coming from customers inquiring about the delivery of their orders, vendors pressing for meetings with the buyer. She is reaching for the outgoing folder when her side vision catches an unfamiliar character who enters the front door and approaches the counter. He is slightly built. His soft, thin-bearded face suggests a young man in his late teens. Trish sees the ear studs and quickly assumes he is looking for a job. She grabs the folder holding blank job applications and approaches the counter.

"May I help you?" she asks, internally cringing at the sight of ceramic-tunneled lobes.

"Hope so. Looking for a Mr. Cornelius."

She hears an accent that says this stranger is not from around here.

"Which one?"

"Believe the name is Spike. Spike Cornelius."

"I'm not sure he is available at the moment. Is there something I can help you with?"

"Naw, it's personal. Just need to talk a minute. Ma'am, if you wouldn't mind, would really like to see him. Come a long ways and just want to speak a moment."

"Would you be looking for a job, for employment? I can help you with that. We're not hiring at the moment, but I can give you one of these applications to complete and we can keep it on file, just in case something comes up."

"Na, thank you, ma'am. S' not a job 'm after, zackly. S' more personal, like I said."

"Let me see what I can do. Excuse me for a moment. You can take a seat over by the window and wait. I'll be right back."

Trish makes her way down the side hall, through the double doors, and down the ramp to the pressroom, where Spike is leaning over an electrical motor on the floor that has been pulled from a nearby press.

"Spike, there is someone up front asking for you. He is a bit persistent. Says it's personal. I've tried to wave him off, but I don't want to be rude. He's probably looking for a job and I've told him we are not hiring, but he is begging. He's just a kid. And he has a bit of an accent I can't quite place. What shall I tell him?"

"Tell him I'll be out in about five minutes after I slide this motor back in place."

❧

Fifteen minutes later, I enter the reception area wiping my wrists with a shop towel as I spot the visitor slumped in a side chair by the front window.

"Are you the one looking for Spike?"

Quickly standing, the stranger extends his hand. "Uhum. You Spike Cornelius?"

"As I live and breathe. How can I help you?"

"My name is Jerome, and I was sent here to give you this letter."

He hands over a faded, well-worn, sealed envelope. I flip it over to the address side and read in cursive writing my own name: "Spike Cornelius, Verona, Georgia." I notice the envelope has neither a stamp nor postmark and no specific address other than the town and state.

I hold it in my hand with a questionable glance toward the stranger, who responds with a shrug and replies,

"Just told to deliver to you and stay with you till you read it."

I rip open the edge of the envelope and pull out a folded collection of pages. On the top is a letter.

Dear Spike,

My hope is that this letter finds you in good health. It has been many years since we connected. Perhaps you remember. At least, I hope you do. It was during Mardi Gras 1997. Seems fate brought us together. I shall never forget those weeks we shared as you looked for work and I waited tables at The Quarter Chateau. We parted abruptly and only after you had been gone for six weeks did I realize I was pregnant with your child, a son, whom I named Jerome Cornelius Hayden. I have instructed him to find you and to deliver this letter to you.

I have been diagnosed with terminal ovarian cancer and do not expect to live much longer. I need to close out my final days knowing I have done my best to connect Jerome with his birth father. He is a good kid. I hope you can help him.

I still think fondly of you and our time together, even after all these years. I hope the years have been more kind to you than to me.

Still, with all my love,

Sybil Hayden
June 4, 2014

P.S. I have enclosed a copy of his birth certificate so you will know
this is not a hoax. Neither is it an attempt to blackmail you. I
just want you to know him, and him to know you. I hope you can
help our son. SH

I feel my knees go weak. My trembling fingers move to the final
page and my eyes scan the official copy of a birth certificate. The
record reads:

Oschner Health System, New Orleans, Louisiana
Date of birth: January 2, 1998
Mother's Name: Sybil Hayden
Father's Name: Spike Cornelius
Address: Unknown

The room tilts a bit as I look up from the documents in my hand.
Jerome hands me a newspaper clipping, folded and frayed around
the edges. I open it and silently read:

The Advocate, Baton Rouge. The funeral rites for Mrs. Sybil Hayden
Broadus were conducted by Father Joseph Conrad of St. Joan of Arc
Chapel, Baton Rouge, July 17, 2014. Mrs. Broadus passed away
July 15, 2014, after a long but courageous battle with cancer.
She is survived by her three children, Jerome Cornelius Hayden,
Thomas Kincaid Evelone, and Meredith Savannah Hodges, all of
Baton Rouge, and three stepchildren, Richard C. Peebles, Theodore
R. Peebles, and Vickie B. Conway, all of Shreveport. Mrs. Hayden
was a long-time employee of Richman Textiles, Inc. Memorial gifts
can be sent to the American Cancer Society or the Hospice of Our
Lady of the River, Baton Rouge.

I attempt to hand the obituary clipping back to Jerome, but he holds
up his hands to indicate the document now belongs to me. I fold
it carefully with the letter and place both in the envelope. I stand
speechless for a moment, staring first at the floor, then briefly into

the green eyes of Jerome before coming to my senses.

"Jerome, please step back to my office with me."

He follows me through the pressroom to the back corner room with plate-glass half walls and takes a seat in front of my cluttered desk amid stacks of samples of papers and inks. I ease into the leather swivel chair on the opposite side.

"Jerome, would you happen to have any identification on you?"

He retrieves his wallet from his hip pocket and pulls out a card, hands it across the desk. I scan the driver's license issued by the Louisiana Office of Motor Vehicles Public Safety Services for the essentials, find a picture ID that resembles the person in front of me, minus the ear studs. The name is Jerome Cornelius Hayden, followed by a Baton Rouge address, DOB 1/2/1998.

"Where are you staying, Jerome?"

"Na place yet, just into town on the bus before dawn."

"How did you find me?"

"Mom didna know your exact whereabouts, but remembered you said you were from Verona, Georgia, somewhere north of Atlanta. She remembered you worked some for a printer in N'Orleans. So I started looking on the web and found a company with the name Cornelius. Took shot this might be it."

"Where is your adopted father?"

"Never really adopted me. S' only my stepfather. In the State Pen at St. Franscisville, life, no parole. There five years now."

I look down at my desktop calendar filled with scribbled notes and random phone numbers, aware that my heart is racing and my gut is courting nausea, thinking of what to say next.

"Jerome, as you can imagine, this is quite a surprise. Unexpected. I had no idea. What do you want from me?"

"Don't know want anything, zackly. Just following Mom's instructions before she died. 'M hungry, though. Not eaten since yesterday breakfast in Montgomery. Could use something to get a burger at McDonalds or something."

"Do you have any means of support?"

"Na, not yet. Hoping you might help on that."

"Tell you what I'm going to do. Here's a twenty, should serve you okay for food for the rest of today and tomorrow morning. I'm going to book you a room at the Motel 6 just eight blocks back toward the interstate. The room will be in your name. Let's meet at IHOP just a block from there at seven tomorrow morning. Does that sound good to you?"

"That'll work. Thanks. See ya then."

I silently usher Jerome out of my office, through the pressroom and to the front entrance, where we shake hands. Jerome begins walking toward McDonalds. I begin to adjust to a new world as I head back to my office to call Mildred at Motel 6.

Last night, I convinced Melissa that my indigestion required me to spend the night in the recliner, thus avoiding her possible inquisition into my irritability. I could not look her in the eye.

But sleep escaped me. I spent the hours staring into the silent blue digital haze of non-stop infomercials. I recalled what I could of my days with Sybil. I remembered the sex. I couldn't remember the jobs, or the places we had slept. I recalled our fight over my jealousy—my interpretation of her flirtation differing from her assessment—and that she was being harassed by the biker at the end of Louie's Bar. I recalled she had a serpent tattoo coiled around her left bicep. I glanced down at my left forearm and find a replica. I stared at my right forearm and detected the faded outline of Sybil, a blue name inside a red heart—carefully camouflaged with an indigo design.

My mind drifted to all the other women, before and since, and pondered how wide my genesis might be spread across the south. The thoughts of my indiscriminate procreation led me back to my current dilemma. What should I tell Melissa? And when? Should she be in on any discussions with Jerome? Last evening, I also entertained what it might take to just make Jerome go away without anyone knowing of his arrival.

I had left the house and drove up to the lake and around the hills as the sun bubbled up from the morning haze. As the pavement hummed beneath my F-150, I imagined multiple scenarios and played each out to its conclusion. One thought to make it all go away was to simply eliminate Jerome permanently, either at my own hands or with the aid of some connections I could make in Atlanta. But my conscience would not entertain this option for more than a mile. I tried to place myself in Jerome's situation. I imagined that what might be most helpful would be an unofficial inheritance, a financial handout of some amount, offered on the condition that Jerome would leave Georgia and never come back. Additional miles of thinking unfolded the nightmares of an ever-escalating blackmail. I pull into the parking lot of the IHOP mentally and physically exhausted. My sleepless night is taking its toll. After a few moments in the slot at the far end of IHOP's parking lot, I exit my pickup with a plan.

Just inside the first entrance, I find Jerome seated on the bench, dressed in the same clothes as the day before. The hostess ushers us to a booth in the back corner and takes our order with coffee and juice. While we wait for our breakfast, we exchange light talk about the conditions of the motel room, Jerome's choice of dinner the previous evening at Sonny's Barbecue, and the weather differences between Baton Rouge and North Georgia.

Cutting up my pancakes into diamonds, I direct the conversation to more specifics. "Jerome, what are your plans?"

"Don't have any. Need work. Love to find a job. Just get by, day to day, ya know?"

"Do you plan to stay around here or move on?"

"All depends on you, I guess. Ya want me to leave, I understand. Ya have yah home n' family all set up here, all nice and neat. Don't want to cause ya no trouble. Here 'cause of mom's wishes, that's all."

"If you didn't stay here, where would you go? What would you do?"

"Don't know, zackly. Thought 'bout enlisting in military, but not sharp on gitten m' legs blown off for sake of oil n' gas. Also thought 'bout going to community college, but don't have any idea what I'd study. And don't know how to pay for it. I like to study. Done pretty good in high school. Wouldn't know it by my GPA, but I kinda breezed by without much effort."

"I've got an idea. I know the manager of this place and could probably get you a job here. You could catch your breath, so to speak, and figure out what you want to do. I could come up with the deposits and the first month's rent for a small apartment somewhere in town to help you get your feet on the ground. Would you be interested in that?"

"Most def! What's catch?"

"The catch is that we keep the facts of our relationship just between us for the time being. I need to sort out how to address my past with my family. You understand? I'm not trying to deny what is. I'm just trying to get my head around all this."

"And if I don't keep this quiet?" Jerome queries, looking down at his empty plate.

"You don't want to go there! Believe me." I stir my coffee vigorously, splashing the brew over the edge and down the side of the cup.

"Spike, I'll take your offer. Thanks."

CHAPTER THIRTY

JON

S tanding in line at the post office, I hold the package Marsha has carefully wrapped in grocery bag paper and labeled for delivery to my mother in Alabama. As I wait behind a local farmer shipping what appears to be a case of muscadine jam, I catalogue the feelings I am having at this moment. I am grateful for Marsha's attention to these family courtesies, but curious about just what it is I am mailing—a present to my mother. I am feeling guilty, that somehow I am missing an important date that is connected to this gift. The calendar behind the postal clerk shows it is June 29, 2015. This date is not near my mother's birthday. It is not my birthday. It isn't my deceased father's birthday or the date of his death five years ago. It's too late to be Mother's Day. Is it an anniversary day? Anniversary of what?

Why did she give me this package? Why did she insist I take it to the post office when she could have easily done this herself? Is she subtly telegraphing me that I am supposed to be doing something without telling me what it is I should be doing?

I shake the box for a hint. It is slightly heavy for its size. Perhaps something ceramic, a bundle of books—not cookies or cake because there are no oily spots on the light tan paper. The lady behind me clears her throat loudly, which causes me to notice that the farmer is now four feet advanced and I need to close the gap in the line. The forward shuffle breaks my search for answers to the mystery in the box.

I am thinking of my mother, with whom I spoke last week, but have not visited since Thanksgiving last year. I recall the spread at the table, not like it used to be; nearly the same food I grew up with, but a different arrangement. Some of the same dishes, but some new dishes added. Same family members in the same seats, except the head of the table, where my second stepfather Collins had presided over the carving of the turkey. He was holding the very knife my father once wielded with great ceremony. My namesake could whittle clean all the meat from a wishbone while still in place within the fowl's breast without breaking the mystical promising joint. It contrasts with Collins' pile of shredded turkey muscle, with no attention to separating the dark from the white. I sigh and deeply miss my dad right now.

The cough from behind alerts me that Fred at the parcel window is waiting on me.

After I make a myriad of choices—insurance, overnight, next day, same week, next month—I hope I told the truth that the package contained no liquids or explosives. I choose to insure it for $500 because I have no idea what is inside. I pay the $52.32 with a debit card and turn to make my way across the marble floor toward the entrance.

"Pastor Jon, good morning!" comes a low-pitched call across the room. I look up to see Reggie standing in line holding a large manila envelope.

"Waiting to send some certified mail" he emphasizes with his package. "Got time for a cup of coffee?"

"Sure. I'll take the time. I'll get us a seat next door at Rhonda's."

"Actually, it is good I ran into you here. I was hoping we could have that coffee in your office, if you still have the time."

"I don't have any appointments," I lied then mentally kicked myself for yielding too quickly my morning hours for sermon preparation to one more interruption that would surely add more pressure to my Saturday sermon scramble finish. "Sure, meet you there in about fifteen minutes. I'll have the coffee ready."

Reggie's arrives forty minutes later and loudly blames the postal service employees for their civil service pace of production and his own request to mail a certified packet.

"Thanks for seeing me, again, on such short notice. Today's a tough one. That letter was to the broker managing the sale of my business. It contained my commitment to move forward with the sale and it starts the clock ticking again. I have just thirty days to agree on a final price, my exit plan, and any role I might play when we turn over the business to the new owner-manager."

"Is this a 'no exit' position for you?" I ask, sipping from my favorite mug.

"Pretty much. It means I have cashed the $100,000 in earnest money issued by the buyer and I would be in breach of contract if I backed out or delayed the deal. We have a range of issues to finalize before the final contract sale, but I would say it is pretty much a done deal. At least it means I have made the tough decision to sell. Still working on the final price, which depends on how much I want to stay involved with the business, how the purchase will be spread out over how many years, and my understanding of all the tax consequences of this sale."

"So, you are at peace with this decision?"

"To start the process of getting out? Some days, yes. Some days, no."

"So, what's the measurement today? Yes? No?"

"I'm at peace with the deal being offered at several levels. I am being offered a fair price, actually a bit more than I expected, which will allow Bonnie and me to travel a bit more in retirement, pay off our mortgage, and purchase a second home, a condo over at Hilton Head."

"But I hear a hint that there may be more that is less peaceful."

"Indeed, you are perceptive, Pastor." Reggie reaches for his cup and slowly moves it to his lips, sips slowly, and leisurely returns it to the side table.

"The problem with Spike will not go away. His lawyer is threatening mine with a court-ordered injunction to delay or cancel the sale if his terms are not met. And the document I signed and sent off today committed me to coming to final terms with the buyer within thirty days or the deal is off."

"So, what is the sticking point between you and your brother?"

"He wants what I consider to be a boatload of money—*my* money, from *my* company—as a part of the final deal."

Reggie's face turned an angry red as he continues.

"Remember how I told you he feels entitled to a huge share of the sale price, and I disagree. He still seems to forget how he abandoned his father and me years ago. Demanded his share then and there, with no consideration for how it affected us. Father had to take out a line of credit on the company, postpone the purchase of several pieces of equipment, just to pay him to get out of our hair. He was causing such a ruckus in the community. Sullying our father's reputation with his drinking, and carousing, and screwing anyone who would stand still long enough."

His hands are trembling as he reaches again for his coffee cup, splashing some drops on the side table.

Lowering my mug to my lap and leaning back slightly, I accept the responsibility of dialogue. "You've mentioned frequently what Spike's demand could cost you. And you've referenced several times how you think he hurt your parents. But I sense there is more to this for you than some amount of money and or your parent's sacrifice."

Reggie continues to clutch his cup, trying to stifle his trembling. With reddening eyes holding back tears, he whispers, "The truth is…I can't stand my brother. I only tolerate him."

Time is suspended for several seconds, Reggie and I frozen in our seats as in a Rockwellian pose. I ponder what to do next, and not knowing, call on my training and self-discipline to do nothing and let the silence do its best work. Then I notice Reggie's head drop slightly, his chin to his chest, the coffee cup rolls out and spills, and his chest and head are in a rapid rhythmic tremble. No tears are streaming from his face, but it is obvious to me that my friend is weeping, sobbing, wallowing in shame but releasing, confessing what he had too long held inside.

I continue to do what I think is best, which is nothing, other than to be present in this moment. I whisper a reply. "It's okay, Reggie. It's okay."

Reggie's attempts to compose himself by focusing on the coffee spilled onto my oriental rug, quickly apologizing for the mishap. Grabbing the box of tissue from the side chair, he slides to his knees, dabbing wads of soft paper not to his face but to the stains on the rug. I slip down beside him, following Reggie's example.

"I'm so sorry, Pastor Jon, for making such a mess. I'll have this professionally cleaned for you."

"Reggie, this is no problem at all. Not to worry."

I dab a bit more, turning the white tissue brown before tossing it toward the nearby wastebasket. I rise and offer my hand down to Reggie, and we both stand together, facing each other. Avoiding eye contact, Reggie quickly turns his back to me and starts to move towards the door. But he stops abruptly when he feels my hand on his right shoulder.

"Reggie, would you like to talk about this more?"

"I don't know, Pastor," he speaks toward the door. "I don't think I can right now. Not just yet."

CHAPTER THIRTY-ONE

Although it is raining, the drive down GA 400 is not that bad for a late-morning commute as I make my way south toward Johns Creek. I called yesterday and arranged to meet my good friend, Aaron, who is also our personal financial advisor. We had already met, all three of us, last month, to review the Boatwright's financial plan and progress toward college funds for our children and our retirement some way-too-distant time in the future. Today, I just want a private, peer-to-peer discussion over lunch to pick Aaron's brain for some insight and advice that has nothing to do with our personal investments. Taking the exit at Cummings toward Johns Creek, I reminisce how this connection with Aaron started.

It was about ten years ago, when I attended a workshop for clergy at Young Harris College. Aaron was the keynote speaker. I was impressed with Aaron's ability to see the crossover of daily finance and business with the daily experience of faith and spirituality. Today, I cannot recall the exact subjects in those workshops, but it was the segue for Aaron to become our family financial advisor. At that time, Aaron was the sole proprietor in his two-room office on a back floor of a two-story office center in Alpharetta. I had admired the entrepreneurial spirit of this former Presbyterian pastor-turned-tax preparer. I remember the start-up name of that company: A.I. Grisham Financial Services, and how disappointed Aaron was when the monster American International Group became entangled in the 2008 credit collapse and government bailout scandal. Some folks thought AIG stood for Aaron's company, so he rebranded it as Grisham's Wealth Management.

Aaron began his business back in the 90s, after nearly twenty years as a senior pastor throughout North Georgia. He joined his old seminary roommate, Richard Cory, from Rome, Georgia, and started a business focused on tax preparation for clergy. Now that business is a full-service financial office with dozens of employees and located in one of the classiest professional complexes in Johns Creek.

I drive past the business campus and notice the massive sign on the side of the building broadcasting Grisham's name. Two miles further south toward Atlanta, I arrive at the St. George Country Club, where Aaron has made reservations for us in the dining room. In the parking lot, I notice how my white Ford Five Hundred contrasts with the black Benz 500 on the left, the white Land Rover to the right, and the brilliant shiny Tesla facing me. Although I feel out of place, I call to mind the memory of my last meal here as Aaron's guest, the fork-tender filet mignon. Can't get that in Verona.

After we order our meal, and have a few exchanges about weather and updates on the families and plans for summer vacations, I get to the point of my request for this lunch conversation.

"Aaron, I deeply value your insight as both my financial advisor and as one who has served in the pastorate. You seem to be able to see through some of the conflicts and disconnects that surface when money and faith are discussed. I've been struggling with some issues in my parish along these lines and would welcome your feedback."

"I'm a bit rusty on the theology and seldom go to church anymore, but I'll be glad to listen, Jon. What's on your mind?"

We receive identical Caesar salads, and simultaneously help ourselves to warm bread and honey butter.

"As I shared with you before, I am working on my doctorate at Epworth and my project focus is how ministry might effectively intersect with the business world. I'm having some success as far as my proposal and write-up of that project, but I'm stuck on some issues that all this has stirred up. The most dominant question bugging me is just how far I should go as a pastor."

I take a moment to sip the sweet tea and Aaron does likewise, waiting for more information from me. "What's at stake, Jon?"

"I feel my calling is at stake. When I decided to enter the ministry, I thought my mission was to look out for the poor and the disenfranchised. I feel I do that in my sermons, my pastoral care, and in leading my church. But I also find I am being pulled, maybe even pushed, to look at more than the just those who sit in the so-called poorer side of the church aisle. I see individuals and families in pain on both ends of the economic spectrum, but it seems to come from vastly different sources.

"I have this fear. A fear that if I start to pay attention to people who are wealthy and successful, I will neglect my calling to serve the poor. I feel I might corrupt myself, become the church pontiff obsessed with lining the coffers of the cathedral, living in luxury at the expense of others. Do you hear what I'm trying to say, but probably not doing a good job explaining it?"

At that moment, the runner brings our main course selection. He sets before me the sizzling hot plate—a marvelous presentation of the very heart of beef, the filet mignon, charred slightly on top and bottom, sitting in its own juice, waiting for my fork to begin its consumption. Sides of asparagus and richly buttered mashed potatoes are placed between us, as Aaron receives his main selection: grilled tilefish.

"I think I hear you, Jon. And I think I heard a question earlier, but it was not clear. What is the question?"

I bite into my fork-cut chunk of steak and for a moment lose the train of conversation as my taste buds revel in aged medium rare beef. I don't want to waste my tongue just now in mere conversation. I slowly chew my food, trying to appear that I am thinking about what Aaron has asked and what my reply will be.

"Aaron, I think my question is a simple as this: How far should I go in ministering to those who have it all?"

Aaron lifts a fork laden with delicate white fish and, placing the morsel in his mouth, smiles at its delicate flavor. Raising his eyebrows, staring directly into my eyes, he replies, "As far as your calling takes you!"

We both enjoy another bite from our plates. Aaron continues.

"As I see it, Jon, as ministers of the Word, both Old and New Testament, we have easily claimed the call of the prophetic voice, to speak on behalf of the poor. And as leaders of the church which ordained us, we have taken up the cloak of social activist for the sake of the poorest in our society. Our seminaries instilled this in our pastoral psyche. Over the past forty years, we've done a pretty good job of shining light on all those rich cockroaches we believed have been the source of the disparity between the richest and the poorest in our culture—the so called one percent. So successful, I believe, that we have run off the new wealthy, left them in the cold, like children wandering in the wilderness."

Taking another bite of tilefish then wiping his chin with his linen napkin, Aaron goes on.

"According to the latest studies, about eighty percent of the people you and I perceive to be wealthy have no experience being wealthy. Look at us. Eating the finest food in one of the finest restaurants in North Georgia. My parents and grandparents would not believe food could be prepared like this. And they would straight out have a cardiac arrest if they had to pay the tip, not to mention the tab.

"As I help myself to another slice of this fabulous bread, look around you without being obvious, like you are looking for our waiter, and take notice of the people dining in this place."

I quickly glance in half circles to the left and right as Aaron butters his bread and takes a bite. I look back at Aaron, quizzically.

"What do you see, Jon?"

"I see a variety of people, all strangers to me, but mostly middle-aged or older, a few thirty-somethings, all nicely dressed in either business attire or golf outfits sitting at linen-covered tables, sipping wine or cocktails and eating a nice lunch. A few are eating alone, but most of them are in groups of people they seem to know. What should I be seeing? Am I missing something?"

"Of the nearly two dozen people eating here, I can see that about one-fourth of them are either my clients or part of my social or business network. I would guess that ninety percent of the diners in this room are in the upper five percent when it comes to net worth, some as high as the top one, and a few I know who are one-half per-centers.

"So, if we apply the eighty percent statistic, about twenty people in this room are wealthy, but have no experience in being wealthy. In other words, their parents or grandparents were not wealthy and they have no mentors to guide them in the land of wealth other than the people sitting across from them or playing golf with them. It is the blind leading the blind.

"Newly minted from generations wandering in the wilderness, now immigrants inhabiting the land of milk and honey and not a clue on how to live in this environment.

"What's more interesting, according to studies done on this matter, is that most of the wealth represented in this room will not make it to the next generation, and only twenty percent of it will ever make an impact on the grandchildren. It will all be gone! As the old adage quips, 'Shirtsleeves to shirtsleeves in three generations.'"

We wave off dessert but each of us agree to a cappuccino and we sit silently for a few moments to absorb what was just said. The irony of our own position in this socio-economic imbalance is not lost on us.

"Aaron, what you are saying about inheritances is dead-on; it is at the heart of what is puzzling me at the moment in my own parish ministry, in fact."

"Go on"

"I have an inheritance issue in my congregation. Actually two inheritances, within the same family. An early inheritance, and more recently, a later inheritance. My question is how many claims can you defend in a family inheritance?"

"I need more background than that to give you an answer. "

"Okay. We both understand the risks that North Georgia is a small world with lots of family and business ties, and that we both have professions that expose us to confidential information. I'm going to risk the possibility of sharing something about someone we both might have in common but I'll still try to disguise the situation somewhat.

"Johnny Rebel as a young man gets a burr up his butt and has a falling out with his old man, demands and gets his share of the family estate and splits town. He blows his inheritance in short order and comes crawling back to Daddy, who takes him back, including re-employing him in the family business. The family business grows over the next two decades, tripling in size, before Daddy dies and leaves the business to Mommy and the oldest son, Faithful Frank. Mommy dies, and now the business is up for sale at a handsome profit for Faithful Frank, but Johnny Rebel is threatening an injunction on the deal because he feels he is not getting his fair share.

"The law and contracts are on the side of Faithful Frank, but it could get really messy if it goes to court. Faithful Frank is a basket case, thought he had his final years of retirement all planned out with the sale of his inherited business. He's coming to me for advice, and I can't imagine arguing over a few million dollars. Transactions in the millions boggle my pastor-salary mind. Seems to me there should be enough to share so everyone is happy. But what do I know?"

"Sounds like I read about this story somewhere recently. Oh, yeah, a few months ago, in the Gospel. They call it the story of the prodigal son." Aaron grins then glances down at the check, adds a tip to round it up to $175.00, enters his *St. George Club* number and signs his name. He motions the waiter to do a second round of cappuccinos, and continues.

"Everyone wants to jump on the elder son's case because he's not all happy about the reunion party Dad is throwing for the repentant son. There are reasons the son is not happy, and what you are experiencing is that parable played out in real life, just twenty or thirty years later."

I go into further detail.

"Yeah, you are right-on. Never thought about it that way. In my case, both sons are all about what they think is justice. The older son thinks justice was served when hotshot brother took his wad away from the family account and blew it without regard to the consequences of the family. It took them years to build back up from that loss. Now the younger son thinks he is the reason there is such a big success in the company, why it is for sale at such a high price. And he believes he should be compensated for his contribution to the value of the family business."

"Jon, what you have here is a classic case of the world of grace crashing headlong into the quest for justice. I see it frequently in my line of work. I see it in politics. I see it in finance. I see it in the courts and laws we try or fail to pass. I see attempts at it being addressed everywhere. Everywhere, except church.

"The church is all about grace. Forgiveness to the repentant. Reconciliation in the differences of minds and values. But the church comes up short, seemingly ignores the consequences of grace long-term. Don't get me wrong about grace—my whole theology was and remains based on the concept of grace—but it does have its costs. Most pulpits proclaim the cost of grace is spent on a cross with a dying prophet as some substitution sacrifice to cover a world of sins. But there are other consequences to exercising grace.

"Grace is exercised at the expense of justice. Folks, like your older son, are torn between an obsession with justice and the release in grace. In the classical prodigal son story, my imagination takes hold of what is going on in the mind of that older brother. The older brother is not happy with the party. This moment of exhilaration that the rebel son is back, alive, found, is not the end of the story. His coming back into the fold complicates the entire system of justice, of future values. Business is based on future values. Doesn't matter if it is farming, manufacturing, or service, whether it is private or government. Whatever is expended in the present is done with a future value in mind. Pay now, so the future is better, cheaper, wealthier, happier. This gets all screwed up when justice calculates to guard the future and grace says there is no accounting.

"God, I wish I had a pulpit again! But for the moment, I'll take this table and you as the congregation. Sorry to dump on you, Jon!

"No, Aaron, please go on. I need to hear this."

"If you insist." He grins and then continues, "This is part of what is at the heart of the great divide in our western culture, particularly in our county now. The more progressive, liberal side of our culture and politics wants to correct what they see are the wrongs in our system, the poor captive in cycles of poverty, the immigrants who provide labor no one else will do but have no claim to a new homeland.

"What I have observed—and I am guilty of it, as well—is that as a liberal and progressive, I want grace to abound, particularly when it is not hurting me. I want to raise taxes, particularly if my tax rate is low and will only go up a bit. I want to dictate that someone else dispense grace at my bidding. But what we as liberals do not understand is that someone else's grace is not ours to give. We can only dispense our own. If we legalize an exercise of grace to require another person to exercise it, it ceases to be grace. It becomes a law, and therefore sets up its own resistance. If I want to give away the farm, as long as it's my farm, my grace in giving it away only impacts me. But if it is the family's farm, or some other person's farm I want to give away, that is an entirely different matter. That is me exercising grace at the pain of someone else.

"So, what I suspect might be at play with your older son's case is a struggle between grace and justice. This guy is all about justice. It is, or so he thought, measurable, predictable, consequential. Inheritance in, inheritance out. Grace, on the other hand, is messy, unmeasurable, hard to pin down when it comes to consequences and sharing the results. The younger son is more familiar with grace because he has experienced it, and likes it. So he thinks others should like it, as well. It worked for him, so why shouldn't it work for his older brother? The problem here is that the older brother is lost in the universe of grace. He has no grounding in this concept.

"Which leads to another angle that is at play here, which I cannot go into without giving attention to my sixty-six-year-old bladder, if you have the time?"

"Go ahead, Aaron. This is interesting. I can wait."

Meanwhile, I call my office to explain that I have been detained by a pastoral situation near Atlanta and will not make the three o'clock staff meeting on time; I may be forty-five minutes late. Aaron returns relieved and relaxed enough to redirect his thoughts and to convey his next point.

The club's dining area is empty except for the two of us, as the staff sets up tables for the dinner hour. Settling into his chair, Aaron jumps right into this next point.

"I suspect there is a second issue that might be playing into this challenge between your two brothers' story. It could be that the older brother is damn envious of the younger while at the same time being angry with himself. Over the course of his adult life, unlike his rebel brother, he has opted to play the safe role of homesteader. He has dutifully delayed his gratification until retirement. Now, his full retirement dreams are being threatened again by the reduction of revenue he was planning on. Faithful Frank, as you call him, feels threatened a second time by Johnny Rebel's antics.

"Frank might also be beating himself up for time lost—decades, perhaps—in lock-down self-righteousness that looks like it is going to be less rewarding than expected. He compares his life with his brother's and wishes privately that he had been a bit more reckless and careless in his younger years. That he could have enjoyed not the tragedies but at least some of the pleasures and excitement. His brother has pushed every envelope, taken risks. Sometimes he lost, sometimes he exhilarated in experiences. Frank has played it safe and he might be feeling a life lost in the pursuit of security. His self-denial of risk and adventure could be backfiring on him, and he has no one to blame but himself. He may need to direct some grace inward more than outward."

⌒⌒⌒

While driving back to Verona, I am mentally processing all that I have heard from Aaron. Not just how it applies to the Cornelius brothers, but to all the other members of my flock. And how does it apply to me? Which side do I come down on regarding grace and justice?

I hear myself preaching both, but usually to the exclusion of the other. I like pushing a self-righteous congregation toward the grace presented in the Gospel parables and the suffering of Jesus. But there are times when the Amos in me thrills to preach justice, to condemn poverty in our backyard, to rage against the inequality of our court systems. The Boatwright strains for family justice. And the Jonathan? Jambo prays for grace.

CHAPTER THIRTY-TWO

O n my way to the office Friday morning, I stop by Molly's home to honor her request to drop by for some coffee and pound cake. I notice the Four Seasons Real Estate sign near her front sidewalk. A magnetic addition to the sign brags that the salesperson has this property "Under Contract." The driveway is filled with folding tables overflowing with household goods. At the edge of the drive is a generic sign from Home Depot announcing a moving sale, with handwriting announcing the date and time: "Saturday, 7 a.m. until." I recognize the women helping Molly set out items and label them with price tags. One is from Molly's Sunday school class, and I met the other two helpful neighbors the day of Bill's death. The neighbor closest to me greets me with a kind smile and tells me Molly is expecting me in the kitchen.

As soon as I close the screen door behind me, Molly steps quickly to embrace me with a silent hug. She then motions for me to sit at the table, where a mug waits for my coffee and a freshly sliced pound cake, fresh from the oven, seems to beckon me.

"Wow, Molly. I had heard things were moving quickly for you, but did not realize the pace you are keeping. Bring me up to date!"

"Well, Pastor Jon, it has been a whirlwind the past few months. I did get together with the advisor you recommended, and he helped me get my head around my financial situation. And Joy was just what I needed to get a handle on all the paperwork.

"As you know, the coroner's report came back clean and eventually the insurance companies made good on the policies. But it took both the advisor and Joy to help me put together a plan for going forward. There were far more debts than I had originally known. Bill had taken out two lines of credit on the house, one from his credit union and another from a bank I never heard of. We were all puzzled how he did this without my knowledge and signature until we discovered this house was in his name, though I shared the mortgage. The advisor mapped out my options, which were a shock for me to accept.

"Bottom line, I can't afford to keep this house, so I put it up for sale and got a reasonable price. But it is underwater, has been for a while, so one of the insurance policies will go to getting the debt paid in full and I'll walk away from this house with only a break-even. The advisor then mapped my prospects for income going forward. We looked at several scenarios, including remaining in the area and renting a condo or moving to someplace cheaper to live.

"I've worked out a deal with my sister in L.A.—that's Lower Alabama for you Georgia folks. I'm going to live in her apartment where our mother lived before she passed. There are not many jobs in that area, but I think I can make do with the investments I am going to make. My advisor says I am about three years away from being eligible for drawing Bill's Social Security Benefit, which will make it tight for a while. But Sarah's place will give me time to catch my breath. I'm glad our kids are on their own. Would you like to buy some stuff from my moving sale? I can give you advance pick of anything you want and set it aside for you."

Sipping my coffee and enjoying another piece of pound cake, I relax to take in more of Molly's update.

"Your yard sale is tempting. I'll take a look around later.

"Meanwhile, this cake is amazing, as always. I'm glad you had some help with the advisor and Joy. I'm sure you have had to think really hard to make this major decision. How are you feeling about up-rooting yourself from here?"

"Well, my decision was partly driven by grief, I must admit. This was our house for twenty-four years. Raised our kids here. But this is also a very painful place for me. I cannot go downstairs without looking to see if Bill is there. And the debt on this place, that he did that without my knowledge or permission, has just turned it into an albatross around my neck.

"Frankly, Pastor Jon, I have to confess that I am damn angry at Bill when I think of what happened. I feel guilty about those feelings, but they are there, nonetheless."

"How are you working on that anger, Molly?"

"Well, selling this house to the first offer is one way. Bill would have never made such a quick decision. He would have tried to create a bidding war to get every nickel he could. We listed this house when the kids finished college, but no one would make an offer because he wanted to make a big profit. Now I know why, but didn't then. And I hate to admit this, but since you are my pastor, I guess it is okay. There were moments over the past few months that I just went on a cussing rage, calling him every foul thing I could think of, then breaking down, crying my eyes out in pain at missing him. And, to tell the truth, I gave God a piece of my mind, as well. Lucky me I wasn't struck down by lightning. You might want to move a bit away from me so you aren't collateral damage." She chuckles.

"Molly, Molly, how refreshing you are to my soul. It looks to me like you are taking life by the horns and riding this through with all the gusto you can. I'm glad you and God are having some 'honest to God' dialogue, pardon the pun. Keep it up. It will serve you well, wherever you go."

We continue our conversation for another fifteen minutes, laughing at some of Bill's things Molly is only too glad to sell, and shed a few tears over items that are difficult to part with. I empty my second mug of coffee, offer a prayer of blessing over Molly's unfolding journey, and step back out into the portico, stopping briefly to admire the John Deer 42" deck lawn mower that a neighbor is polishing. I casually lift the tag, which reads, "$500, or best offer," then sigh and walk down the aisle between the tables of tools, camping gear, books on finance and history, dishes of every description, a dozen lamps, and an overstuffed leather recliner.

I ponder if that particular chair will ever fade from my memory.

CHAPTER THIRTY-THREE

S topping by Cornelius Printing to drop off the draft of Sunday's *Order of Worship*, I decide in the moment to see if Reggie is available. If he can drop in on me unannounced, surely I could return the favor. Trish places an intercom page for Reggie to come to the front lobby. When he comes through the swinging double doors, his face confesses a kind of bemused disappointment. He expects a profitable customer, not his pastor. He forces a smile and extends his hand.

"Good to see you, Pastor Jon. Thanks for stopping by."

He waits for me to make a move.

"Just hadn't talked with you for a while, Reggie, and thought I'd drop by to see how you are doing." The ball is now in Reggie's court.

"Come on back, if you got a minute. Actually, it is a good time. Glad to see you. Give me a minute to hand off the delivery list to Spike. Make yourself at home in my office. I'll be right with you."

I make my way to the office as Reggie passes back through the swinging doors, but instead of going to the loading docks, he ducks into the Men's room, locks the door, and looks in the mirror at himself. What he sees is a mess—bloodshot eyes, puffed eyelids, pale skin, areas missed by a hasty razor the day before. He splashes water on his face and wonders what he will tell his priest. Everything is fine, no problems, all is well, tough times, but getting through them? Or should he admit that he is suffering from insomnia, oppressed by his own indecision about what to do with the sale of the business while every delay only increases the agony? Should he share that his wife is putting pressure on him to settle this deal immediately, take the money and run. He concludes that his face will reveal the lie and he remembers he failed acting his freshman year.

"Jon, didn't expect to see you. I know I've been out of pocket the last few Sundays, and shame on me."

"Well, I certainly didn't come by to heighten your guilt, Reggie. It's just that we had some very serious conversations and I've not seen you since. Just checking in to see how you are doing."

"Actually, I've been avoiding you, Jon. A bit embarrassed about myself. Did you get the carpet cleaned? Sorry 'bout that."

"No worries there, Reggie. Our custodian, Harold must have a magic wand at his disposal. You can't even tell anything happened. So, how are you? Any progress in the business proposal?"

"After we talked in your office, the next day, I went to see my attorney, who sent me to his attorney friend in Atlanta, a specialist in mergers and acquisitions. I got an appointment right away and we met. I explained the situation and he gave me his insight and advice—which, by the way, is not cheap, at five hundred an hour. I'll have to charge the church a little extra on this week's printing order to make up for it." He chuckles, revealing he still retained a sense of wry humor, but also another subtle reminder to me that The Hill printing bill never covers the true charges for all the services we receive from Cornelius.

I grin, acknowledging the indirect reminder, and remain silent but watchful, inviting Reggie to go on.

"Jon, according to this Atlanta expert, I have three choices. I can ignore Spike's threat and move forward with the sale, but risk his legal course of seeking a court injunction on the sale. Legally, in this attorney's option, the documents pertaining to the ownership of the company will most likely prevail, plus the documents surrounding the estate settlement. But it would take a while for that to wind its way through the courts for it to eventually be in my favor. I can easily win the case, but it would be expensive, probably, at more than five hundred per hour in legal fees."

"And your other options?"

"I could use my owner discretion and allow Spike to have immediate shares in the company, an action that would entail some tax issues and other consequences. This would allow Spike to receive part of the proceeds from the sale, but allow the sale to move forward with no delay. The buying company does not care where the sale proceeds go, nor who the shareholders are. They just want the company on their books and to start making management decisions as quickly as possible, with existing staff or perhaps new management.

"The attorney suggests a third option, which would be a memorandum of agreement between me and Spike. This memo would be legally binding and could promise that I would remain the sole owner of Cornelius Printing, but any sale proceeds after settlement would be split according to a percentage defined in the memo.

"Options two and three are pretty clear-cut. The second option would be recorded in the courthouse records and with the state, and thus be open to the public. It would cost much less than fighting the injunction. The third option would allow everything to be private, and only our attorneys would be privy to the arrangement."

"So, Reggie, which way are you leaning?"

"The last option seems the most reasonable, if we can come to terms. But for the life of me, I just cannot stomach the idea. It seems so unjust. I just boil when I recall all the mess Spike caused years ago, how he bailed on us, put us in debt to pay him off. Now he wants to re-enter the picture with his hand out as though nothing happened, as though I have forgotten about his past. I guess what I want is justice at last."

"Is there any room for fairness?"

"What do you mean, fair?"

"Reggie, I don't want to meddle too far into this, but since you have invited my consult, and shared with me all the history of what has occurred, is Spike's request unfair? After all, you have not denied his role in the success of Cornelius Printing. Am I right?"

"Yes, you are right, damn it!"

"Let me ask something from another angle, if I may?"

"Sure, Preacher, go for it!"

"You explained that your parents, particularly your father, were the ones who allowed Spike to come back home and start all over."

"Yes, actually, both of my parents were equally agreed on that action. They didn't take his actions lightly, but they took him back."

"Why do you think they did that? Did they ever discuss it?"

"Not with me. They just seemed relieved. Happy, in fact, even though he had all these tattoos and substance abuse problems. They didn't consult me. I had no say."

"So, looking back on that period, Spike coming back home. Suppose you *did* have a say."

"I would have said, 'No way. Go find your own way, Spike.'"

I wait a few seconds before responding.

"Reggie, have you ever experienced any grace in your life?"

"What, getting something for nothing? Absolutely not! I've worked for every dime I ever made. I have given my life to this family business, even though there have been times I have hated every minute of every day. And those days are coming around too quickly."

"Your hard work is very evident here, Reggie. What I mean by grace in this conversation is a bit different. It is not necessarily getting something for nothing. It is getting something good when you might not deserve getting it. Have you ever done something wrong and not suffered the full consequences of that action?"

"Can't recall any at the moment, Preacher. What's your point? I married as a virgin, and married a virgin. Been loyal to my wife all these years. Raised our kids to be respected in our community. Took care of Father and Mother in their old years."

"I see your point, Reggie. Just wondering if you ever were on the receiving end of something akin to what Spike received when he came home from his wild escapades.

"From where I sit—and believe me, I am not in your shoes, so I am making no judgments about you—but it looks to me that your attorney has spelled out three options that, if I can put them in my language, sounds like this: You have been presented with the option that is legal, an option that is fair, and an option that is pure grace."

"From what I am hearing, you are caught up in the legal/justice option, and are having a hard time considering either the fair or the grace options. Am I reading you right?"

"Dead on, Preacher. I drive a hard bargain. I believe legal is fair because everyone has the same set of rules to live by. You screw up, you pay the price. You play nice, you work hard, the world is your oyster. There is one thing I am not, and that is someone who gives a damn about the plight of others. I am sick of people who think the world owes them a living or handout. It is ruining our country. And that same attitude is threatening to ruin all the success I have worked for. I've seen it over and over again. You give someone an inch, then they ask for the moon. Look at my situation. Father took the grace route, which was neither fair nor according to law, and look where it got us in the end. 'Sure,' he said. 'Come on home, Spike. We love you. We missed you. Come back into our family as if nothing happened.' And so he did, and we did. He comes back with his head down, his hand out, groveling, and we say, 'Okay, all is forgiven.' Now he stands with his head up, and his hand is still out, saying again, 'Give me what is mine.' But Preacher, it isn't his. He blew his years ago. Doesn't he see that?

"Furthermore, I never, *ever* asked our parents for anything. I did their bidding. Worked hard. Never abandoned them in their old age. I didn't write the trusts that gave this business to me. They did. All nice and legal. And it seems only fair. So, yes, I have little time for grace in business. You can preach it from your pulpit about our souls, about Heaven and Hell, but when it comes to business, it should be all business. Business is business. A deal is a deal. Sometimes you win, sometimes you make some bad calls and you lose. But everyone plays on the same field with the same rules. I'm a baseball fan. You don't play all season with one set of rules for runs, and innings, and outs, for trades and which field you are going to play on, then have another set of rules for the playoffs, and another set for the World Series. No, you play with the same rules from spring training until early November—no exceptions."

"Reggie, I hear your analogy to baseball, and when it comes to baseball, I don't like the differences in the American League and the National League. I think they should be the same. But what is at stake here in your situation is not a World Series, not a game, but lives. Your life. Spike's life."

"Let me correct you, Pastor Jon. What is at stake here is not my life or Spike's life. What is at stake here is business, *my* business, pure and simple."

I realize I am making some ground in getting the issues on the table, but failing to sway Reggie from his arrogance. Looking down and studying the pattern on Reggie's carpet, I think of my next step.

Do I continue to argue, to debate, or bow out and run? I calculate quickly that at this stage in the conversation and the ongoing Cornelius drama, I have nothing to lose. Taking a deep breath to double-check that conclusion, I embolden myself to speak squarely with Reggie who is staring down at the scribbles on his desktop calendar, signaling he is done with this conversation.

"Reggie, you have control of this situation, and in fact, control of this conversation. I do not want to overstep my bounds on this matter. But with your permission, I would like to address something you said just a moment ago."

"If you must… what do you have to say?"

"I thought I heard you say something about the family trusts. I thought I heard you say 'I didn't write the trust that gave this business to me.' Did I hear you correctly?"

"Yes, that's exactly what I said. I didn't write the trusts. My parents did."

"But the way you said it…you said, 'the trusts that GAVE this business to me.'"

"Yeah, and what's your point?

"That's the point. The only point, Reggie."

Reggie's flushed face looks up from his desktop with red, angry eyes that connect directly with mine, then he drops his head to stare again down at the desktop. I get the signal that this conversation is over.

"Reggie, you have some tough choices to make. I'll be praying for you as you try to find what will work best for your peace of mind. Whatever your decision, I will continue to care for you as a friend, and as your pastor."

I slowly rise, then lean over to gently touch Reggie's hands which remain locked in a tight, interwoven grip on the top of the desk. I place my hand briefly on his, then silently turn and walk out of the office.

CHAPTER THIRTY-FOUR

My mind is completely absorbed in what just happened. I rethink what I said and toy with the fear that I might have stepped out of bounds, that somehow I might have been a bit too confrontational with a parishioner who is part of the selection committee that brought me to The Hill. I race through the possible outcomes—a call from the bishop, the loss of the Cornelius family and their giving, the loss of the good discount and printing service The Hill has come to depend on. I steer the Ford Five Hundred into the church parking lot and see a white van, parked right next to my reserved space. As I pull up, the driver of the van slowly exits and his face seems vaguely familiar.

"Pastor Boatwright, George Nelson." The visitor extends his hand toward me.

I respond with a handshake then recall this is one of the families who had caught me after a Sunday morning service asking for a handout.

"Good morning, George. It has been a while. How was your trip to Florida?"

"It was okay. We picked up some jobs as we expected and they got us through the winter and early summer. We're just making our way back north, hope to get to Virginia by tomorrow to begin picking grapes in all those vineyards they've started. Wondering if you could be so kind as to assist us in getting there?"

"Perhaps. I see you are in a different van, a bit bigger and newer than the last time you were through here."

"Oh, yeah. That one died while we were in Plant City. We earned enough to replace it with this. It is a bit bigger, thank goodness, because we have a new baby on board. The younger daughter had her baby and the father is traveling with us. We'd be pretty cramped if we were still in the old one."

"So, George, what do you need?"

"Some food would be nice. Haven't eaten since Tuesday. And we're completely out of gas. Could also use somewhere to stay the night, you know. Get a bath and wash our clothes. Anything you can do to help us out would be greatly appreciated, Pastor Boatwright."

The children and the child-mother are now crawling out of the van, roaming about the empty parking spaces, avoiding eye contact with me.

"Sure, George. Give me a moment. By the way, are you contacting any of the other churches in this area for assistance?"

"Honestly, Pastor Boatwright, yes, but no luck. We stopped at two on the south side of town. One was locked, looked like no one was around, but there were cars in the parking lot. The other said the preacher was out and he had to give the okay for any help they offered. So, we made it to you. You were very kind last fall, and we deeply appreciated all you did for us. Much appreciated. And we hate to come back to you again, but we're desperate. Anything you can do to help us will be graciously accepted."

"Follow me, Mr. Nelson. Let's see what we can do."

I lead the way toward the church office, enter by using my code on the electronic lock, and usher in George, who follows me down the shiny clean hall one step behind, a grime-stained Braves ball cap in hand. Opening the door to the administrative suite, I greet Elizabeth with a quick "Good morning" and then add, "Elizabeth, Mr. Nelson needs some assistance today. Can you please arrange for him and his family to get lunch and dinner at the Tic Toc, and a room with the Patels' and also a tank of gas at Joe's."

"Oh, thank you, Pastor Boatwright. One other thing, could it be possible to get some baby food, some milk, and some diapers for the grandchild?"

"I'll take care of that from our pantry, Jon," Elizabeth intercepts. "Have a seat, Mr. Nelson, and let me make some phone calls."

I reach out to George with a firm handshake.

"Good to see you, George. Elizabeth will take care of you from here. I wish you Godspeed on your journey."

I have learned neither to belabor the point of repeated requests nor to get too upset when those seeking help become a bit forward in asking for more. I am reminded of the little book I read to my small children, *When You Give a Mouse a Cookie.* There are two ways to approach these situations, I remind myself. Get all bothered about the reasons for the situation and try to change the course of the needy, or just respond to the need presented at the moment without being a social worker or a policeman.

As I set my bundle of books and files on the desk, I question what it must do to a man to ask for help. *Does it hurt at the outset of the situation, and then by desperation do you get calloused to your feelings and boldly ask for whatever you can get? Or, does just a bit of you die at each request? And once inside the rut, does it just become a way of life?*

I also ask myself, *am I an enabler? Are we just perpetuating the problem for people like the Nelsons, who seem to arrange their travel from one end of the East Coast to the other based on planned stops at places that give them what they need?* I remind myself that this is the loop of self-conversation that is played in my brain each time someone approaches me and each time I arrange a temporary solution.

CHAPTER THIRTY-FIVE

Marsha Boatwright is awakened by an incoming message on her cell phone. It is from her closest friend, Peggy and the text reads, "Check your paper for an announcement to share with Jon. Congratulations!" She rises from her bed, puts on her robe and slips by the closed door of Jon's study, where he is prepping for his Sunday sermon. Down the stairs and out the front stoop, pulling her hair aside, she reaches down at the curb to pick up the Sunday edition of the *Verona Times*. She stops on the porch, perches on the arm of the wicker lounge to start scanning the paper and finds something that pleases her. She grins, re-folds the paper, tucks it under her arm and re-enters the house.

As the usual Sunday morning around the Boatwright house follows its routine to hold down confusion and meet deadlines, I am the first to arrive at the kitchen table, where I prepare my toasted raisin cinnamon bagel with a thick layer of cream cheese. While I am preparing this delicacy Marsha extends today's newspaper over my left shoulder; she had opened then re-folded to a specific quarter page, which she places on the table beside my coffee mug. Surprised, I scan the print to see what is so important as to have such a private delivery, when my eyes catch my own name.

Boatwright Receives Doctorate

The Conley School of Theology announces the awarding of the Doctor of Ministry to The Right Reverend Jonathan Amos Boatwright, Jr., who is the senior pastor of The Summer Hill Memorial Church, Verona, Georgia. The degree was awarded in graduation ceremonies conducted last Wednesday at the Chapel of Epworth University. Dr. Boatwright's graduate project is titled: "Intersecting the Disciplines of Theology and Business in the Context of the Local Community and Parish." An additional twenty-six candidates also received their Doctorates during the impressive ceremony, which featured the notable Guest Professor of Preaching and Literature, The Right Reverend John Killinger, PhD, as the commencement speaker.

Marsha squeezes my shoulder and kisses me on the neck. "It was a grand day, wasn't it? I still can't believe we have a *doctor* in the house."

I respond with a kiss on her lips then break into a huge grin as she slips back to the kitchen counter. I rarely linger over Sunday breakfast. But feeling confident in my recall of the sermon, I take a moment to open the Sunday paper. It is a glimpse of what it must be like to kick back on such mornings and stroll through the local news.

I glance quickly through the headlines—the county park swimming pool closing being accelerated because of need for repairs, the At-Large County Supervisor announcing her intent to run for re-election. I flip through additional pages to the fifth page, glancing at the editorials and letters from readers. My attention is drawn to the lead editorial.

Another Outside Business Takeover?

The Town Talk is hearing rumors that one of Verona's family businesses is being heavily courted to sell to a firm that has no connections to Verona. One of the cherished qualities of a small town is the local ownership of businesses that support us and which we support. When we purchase services and products from our local businesses, we strengthen the viability of our community. When we buy from our local vendors in Verona, instead of traveling an hour in traffic to make a purchase at one of the mega box stores or malls, we are supporting our community. When we buy down the street from a local vendor and friend instead of purchasing something a bit cheaper online from an international mega corporation, we strengthen our ties of local commerce.

Such community support is even more profound when that local business is owned and operated by our neighbors. Neighbor owner- ship stimulates the local economy, as the profit is poured back into investments here. In a technical sense, we are not the shareholders of local businesses. But we are the stakeholders. When the ownership remains with the people we meet at the grocery store, the coffee shop, and the post office, we all prosper. Local ownership means the profit we produce for each of our businesses will more likely be reinvested in our community. The taxes generated in local sales, the income and capital gains from those who live with us are more likely to have a bigger impact in improving our way of living.

Therefore, it is always disturbing when a local business is being heavily courted by a major national firm. Of course, if you are the owner of such a business, who can blame you for considering an offer that is hard to refuse. It is the way the economy works. Most business owners who develop their businesses over several years dream of the day when a future buyer of the business rewards the hard work of the ownership. We understand that dream. But we wish the dream included the transfer of ownership from neighbor to neighbor. Family-owned and operated businesses are the backbone of our long-term success.

If we look at the list of businesses in Verona today versus the list thirty years ago, we will see an alarming trend. In 1980, nine out of ten businesses were owned and operated by local citizens. Though the number of businesses has grown since then, the number of local businesses has actually decreased. The old family establishments are slipping away to national and international corporations.

While we do not know all the details of a proposed purchase, we hope the owners of all businesses will make every attempt to sell first, if they must sell, to our neighbors. We hope that in some future edition, the news of the change of business ownership announces a local solution so we can keep Verona's commerce thriving for our generations to come.

I sense my blood pressure elevate slightly as I fold the paper and place it beside my napkin. Though no company name is mentioned, Sunday's editorial is clearly an early scoop on the personal business considerations being processed by the Cornelius family.

CHAPTER THIRTY-SIX
SPIKE

As I enter through the double doors at Denny's, I look for Jerome who insisted on meeting me for breakfast. Stepping toward the hostess, I glance across the tables and see Jerome sitting in the far left corner booth, his back to the entrance. I decline the hostess' offer to usher me and make my way to the side of Jerome, who looks straight ahead to the back of the opposite seat, barely acknowledging my arrival. Sitting across the booth, Jerome stares into my eyes. His neck is flushed. Before either one of us speaks, Joanne introduces herself as our waitress. In one rounded motion, she delivers a glass of ice water and an empty cup to me, refills Jerome's mug, then my mug without asking, and inquires if we want to order. I order a Grand Slam Mi-Hammy, over easy, with blueberry pancakes. Jerome motions he will take the same.

"So, what's all this about, Jerome?"

"Been thinking, Spike. Thinking a lot lately. And reading newspapers. Starting to put two and two together. Looks like my ole man is 'bout to cash in on a sale of the print shop. What you going to do?"

"I don't know what you mean. What are you asking?"

"You gonna take your share an' live the good life? Get a place down in Florida? Get a nice house, maybe a boat on the shore?" Jerome's tone is a bit pitched, and snarly.

"Actually, Jerome, this is none of your business."

"Well, I think I want to make it my business. Think I'm due some of what's coming to you, being your firstborn and all."

"So, my firstborn, just how much do you think you are due?"

"Thinking maybe hundred grand set me up nice. I get out of your hair, leave you alone in this community. Be on my way. Keep our relationship our little secret."

"That sounds a bit like a threat, Jerome. Am I hearing you correctly?"

"I think you get the picture."

"So, what if I don't agree with your terms?"

"Well, been thinking of that. You seem to take care to make my presence staying a secret around here. Keeping me holed up in an apartment across town. Avoiding the place where I work. I've looked over this hick town and think it's a dead-end. I want to move on, but I don't have the money. From what I 've heard, the locals are talking about you since the newspaper leaked the news about the print shop for sale. You had the same idea when you were my age. Some of the old folks are telling me you hit your ol' man up for some cash then split. I'm thinking I might do the same."

"And if I don't come up with the cash?"

"Don't think you want me to go there."

"Go where?"

Jerome squirms in his seat, adjusting himself a bit taller, and delivers what sounds to me as a well-rehearsed pitch. "I'd have to let your little secret out. And the first place I would start is with your pretty little wifey."

"I'm afraid that wouldn't work too well for your benefit, Jerome," I calmly reply, looking deep into my own face across the table.

"Why not?" Jerome ups the ante with a bit louder counter.

"Because my 'wifey,' as you call her, already knows about you. I have already told her more about you and where you came from than you know yourself."

Jerome drops his head and looks down into the dark gap between the edge of the table and his lap.

Joanne announces her arrival with a cheery, "Here we are, two Mi-Hammy's over easy with biscuits. Looks like they threw in some grits for free."

She lets our plates find the tabletop with a slight drop, the only sound at this setting for the next thirty seconds.

"In fact, Jerome, not only have I shared everything with Melissa— and I hope you will retain the courtesy from this point forward of using her name instead of my 'wifcy'—we have fully discussed your situation and ours. I thought this meeting would be an update from you to me on your progress, and I was looking forward to hearing how you are doing. But instead, I get not only a shakedown from my son, but a not-so-veiled threat of blackmail. Not a good way to get on my good side, Jerome. You never want to blackmail people who have spent time in prison. They know too many angles on how to wiggle out of jams. Aren't you going to eat your breakfast?"

Jerome looks up with a countenance that admits he is out of his league. He pushes his plate away and looks like he is going to throw up.

In the following two minutes of total silence, I finish my breakfast with an annoyance mixed with an ironic satisfaction. The contrast feeds my indigestion. I slowly place my utensils and napkin on top of my empty plate, then push it toward the edge for Joanne to pick up. I raise my eyes to look at my son, but all I see is the top of his bent-down, buzzed crown. And I wait.

Joanne arrives with the coffee urn for refills and quickly senses she is in the middle of some trauma between two very different-aged men. The silence speaks to her a warning that she best not interrupt and quietly backs away in response to the wave of my hand.

I detect some sniffles coming from Jerome. He starts to leave the booth while avoiding eye contact with me, but I reach out to hold his hand firmly to the table, communicating that there is no quick exit from this confrontation.

"Jerome, I'm ready to talk, and I think you might be ready to listen. At least I hope so."

Spike Junior slides back into the booth, slumping down, looking up with red, watery eyes and a dripping nose. He uses the back of his hands and then his right sleeve across his face to clear away tears as I hand a napkin to him.

"Melissa and I have been talking about you a lot lately, Jerome. And it was her idea, which I had to get up to speed with, to invite you to come and stay with us. We have an extra room that is yours if you want it."

The junior's face wrinkles up in pain, his squinting eyes pushing out teardrops that have no place to go but splash on the edge of the tabletop. He is speechless for several minutes before excusing himself to go to the restroom. While he is away, I receive the check, add a generous tip with cash, then make my way to the restroom as well. I find Jerome staring at himself in the mirror, cold water running in the sink. As I place a hand on his right shoulder, I see two teary-eyed Spikes in the mirror, one looking at himself as the fool, the other with understanding. Does the younger want to go home with the elder?

Without additional words, we exit the restroom, then the restaurant before facing each other in the middle of the handicap parking slot.

There is a pause between us, each wondering who should speak first and what the other would say.

"I'm sorry, Spike."

"And so am I, Jerome. I'm ready to start a new chapter in my life with you, if you are willing."

"I am."

"Here is my address. Melissa is expecting you for dinner at 6:30 tonight. She's fixing her mean meatloaf that is not to be missed. See you there?"

"I'll be there."

CHAPTER THIRTY-SEVEN

JON

Two weeks have passed, and I am at home mowing the lawn as part of my "late arrival to work" routine for Wednesdays. Today's mowing experience is exceptional. I am trying to fine-tune the adjustments for my seating position on a riding lawn mower, a gift left on our driveway last Saturday with a hand-written note attached.

> *Pastor Jon, thanks for all your care for me during these months of adjustments. With your help, I am moving on with my life. I hope you enjoy this. I had it overhauled and a 90-day guarantee on the work. It should be running okay. If you have a problem, Rusty's Mower Repair will take care of anything that needs attention. Thank you, again. Molly.*

I am completing only the second full counter-circle of the backyard when Marsha steps near my path and signals with her hand to her ear that I am needed on the phone. When I cut the motor, she shouts:

"It's Spike, something about Reggie. Needs to talk to you."

In the kitchen, I pick up the receiver from the counter and quickly receive Spike's apology for calling me at home. "No worries, Spike.

What's up?"

"Reverend Boatwright, I'm concerned about Reggie. He's not been around the office since Friday evening, which is totally not like him. I called his wife, Bonnie, but she said he had gone fishing for several days on Lake Lanier. She seemed unconcerned. But Reggie and I always coordinate our time off, and he hasn't said anything to me about being gone. I'm worried."

"Have you called the police?"

"No, not yet. I know you have been helping Reggie through some stuff recently, and I thought I would check with you first. I don't want to get our business in alarm overload by bringing in the cops when it might be nothing."

"So, what can I do for you, Spike?"

"I know I have no right to ask this, but since you are his pastor, if you had the time to check on Reggie I would be grateful. I'd go up to the lake and look for him myself, but we're on a magazine deadline right now and without Reggie, the entire operation is on me. That's another reason this seems strange for Reggie to bug out without talking to me. I did call the marina this morning to see if they knew anything. They said he checked in Friday evening, bought some gas and bait and ice, some food, and that the boat has been out of its slip all weekend. Someone spotted it back in the slip this morning. That's all they know, and they are not volunteering to go check on him."

"Spike, I'll see what I can do. I just happen to have a gap in my schedule this morning, so I'll take a drive down there. I'll let you know if I find anything. But keep me posted if you hear anything. You have my cell number. I'll leave in a few minutes."

"Thanks, Pastor Jon. I really appreciate this."

In the next fifteen minutes, I park the mower in the garage and clear the edge of town headed toward Lake Lanier. During the fifty-minute drive, I ponder the possibilities of what might have happened to Reggie and hope the worst case is only my imagination. My smartphone reminds me of the multiple turns I must take to reach the Inner Banks Marina.

My destination at the lake has become familiar to me over the past two years, thanks to the generosity of Reggie. His houseboat had been the perfect writing studio for putting together the multiple drafts of my doctoral presentation. As I pass through the tall pine thickets on the narrow back roads of Northeast Georgia, I recall my childhood on Lake Thurmond, a two-hour drive to the south. Teenage days of skiing with my high school buddy, Mom's dinners on the deck, fishing all night for white striped bass and crappie.

As I pull into the parking area at the marina, I re-orient myself to the park-like fishing camp. I am surprised by the low water level, nearly four feet below average, and the wide spans of bleached clay ground extending thirty yards from the grassy line of the bank to the water line. A recent drought has brought a harshness to this retreat setting. Finding the correct dock section, I make my way down the walkway, then the ramp slanting down to a flotilla of two dozen boat slips filled with a few run-a-bouts, some ski and bass boats, but mostly houseboats that range from perfection in luxury to shacks floating on water. About thirty feet ahead, I spot *The Latest Edition*, Reggie's pride and passion, a vintage Stardust Cruiser, 52 foot, with twin in/outboard motors, stateroom, fully equipped galley, and an ample fishing deck.

As I come even with the bow and portside, I am shocked by what I see. Dozens of empty Miller Lite cans are scattered across the green artificial turf cover of the fishing deck, some rocking with the gentle motion of the vessel and others crushed. An empty fifth of Myer's Rum is tossed on the pile of lines, and a depleted liter of Cutty Sark rolls back and forth between a stack of beer cans and a crusty minnow bucket. An overturned ice chest, with a broken hinge, gapes open to reveal watery trash and debris from snack crackers. A crushed deck chair sits askew. Several broken fishing rods are tangled in filament line under a dip net.

I lean toward the deck and holler, "Reggie? Reggie?" but receive no reply.

I step from boardwalk to deck carefully so as not to disturb anything. Trying to peer through the front sliding glass doors for any signs of life, I notice dried blood on the edge of the entrance and door handle. I hear buzzing and realize there are dozens of flies on the inside of the glass, seeking an escape toward daylight. I holler once again, and again no reply. Sliding the glass door open, a rancid odor bellows toward me, flipping my stomach.

"Reggie!"

No answer.

Carefully noting not to touch anything if I can avoid it, I hold my breath and take one step in. I listen and detect what I cannot hear. There are no motors running, no air conditioning. The air is both putrid and hot. With risk to my gag reflex, I try one more summons.

"Reggie, are you here?"

"What the hell?" is a reply from somewhere back in the bowels of the water cruiser.

Suddenly, I detect a human silhouette standing in the dim hallway between the stateroom and the galley. "Who are you?" the shadow asks.

"Reggie, it's me, Pastor Jon."

"Oh, God!" is the shouted reply. "You're the last person I need to see me like this."

Reggie steps into the natural light filling the forward seating area. His eyes are bloodshot, and a crimson and white-streaked tank top is wrapped like a turban around his wild-haired head. Stripes of blood have made their way down a sunburned chest where they stalled and clotted some time ago. He leans to the left, using the refrigerator to support him as he stands on his left leg, his right leg pulled up to avoid pressure from the floor. He is wearing only boxer shorts, but a Hawaiian shirt is wrapped around his right thigh, with a canvas belt holding the makeshift bandage in place.

"What the hell has happened to you, Reggie?"

"Better question, Pastor, is what has not happened to me. I've cracked my scalp, finally stopped the bleeding. But my leg is giving me fits."

I realize that some of the redness in Reggie's legs is more from a feverish infection rather than sunburn.

"Reggie, let's get you to a hospital right away. I'll drive you in my car."

"Wait, Preacher! Where are you taking me? I can't go home like this."

"I understand. Let's just get in the car. I'll help you up the ramp and dock. We can go to an ER in Gainesville or Duluth."

After assisting Reggie outside the houseboat, I further secure the lines to the docking and lock the cabin. After we are in the car and headed toward Gainesville, I remain silent to allow Reggie to take the lead in explaining the last five days. It takes about ten miles before the volunteer confession trickles forth.

"Preacher, you're probably wondering what the hell is going on with me. How did you find me?"

"Spike called me this morning concerned about you. Said you were missing in action, and he couldn't leave the shop because of the deadlines this week. He gathered from your wife that you were up here fishing, so he asked me to check on you. Good thing I did, huh?"

"Good thing."

Another mile of silence.

"So, what's going on with Reggie?"

"My life dumped on me, Preacher. A week ago today, I got the bad news that Gannett cancelled the sale contract. They got some rumors that the deal was going to be threatened by an injunction and got cold feet. I am sure it wasn't a rumor. That Spike was actually toying with the idea. Don't know how far he got, but it doesn't matter now. The deal is dead. The buyers have moved on to other options.

"Then just about forty-eight hours later, I got served with papers. The Sherriff's deputy walked right into my office at the shop, stood in front of my desk, shoved an envelope in my hand, and said, 'Sir, you have been served,' then left. I had no idea what he was talking about. I thought it was papers for an injunction, which seemed delayed justice, if you know what I mean. Turns out the papers were for a divorce, initiated by my wife. Also turns out she had been working that angle for six months, and was going to spring it on me after the sale of the business so she could be sure and get her fair share of the proceeds. When it turned out the sale was busted, she said, 'What the hell, I want out.'"

"So, Preacher, I kind of lost it. In three days, I lose the sale of my business and my plans for retirement. And I lose my wife, the main reason I was going to retire. So, I just came out to the lake to contemplate my next steps.

"I just thought I would show them all, Spike and the bitch, and just kill myself. But I couldn't even do that right. Had it all planned out to take some pain medications and drown myself in booze, but got so sick I threw it all up before it could take effect.

"Then I thought about a Plan B, which was to just go out in the lake at night and jump overboard. Which I did. But I didn't go out deep enough. Jumped in, expecting to be in about fifty feet of water, but suddenly realized I was in only eight feet deep. On top of that, I happened to land on a submerged stump and ripped my leg open something fierce. I was in too much pain to die.

"So, I came back to the surface, pulled myself onto the deck, and tied myself up to stop the bleeding. By that time, I had changed my mind, didn't want to die in such pain, so I tried to make it back into the dock to get my leg fixed. It was really dark getting around the coves and I lost my way a few times. I was out on the deck while the boat was moving at about a trolling speed. I was looking out into the darkness when *blam*, the boat hit a shallow area and a rock. It slammed so hard, it knocked me down on my face and my head hit one of the cleats on the deck, knocked me out cold for several minutes with the engine still running, boat jamming further into the rocky shore. When I came to, blood from my split scalp was everywhere. The front hull was intact but all beat up. I stayed put just drifting until daybreak, then slipped into the marina and drank whatever I could put my hand on just to dull every pain in my body and soul. And then you showed up. Lucky you, huh?"

"No, Lucky YOU."

CHAPTER THIRTY-EIGHT

I t is Wednesday morning and I am at my writing desk, deep into my research for Sunday's sermon, when Elizabeth's voice over the intercom breaks into my thoughts. "Dr. Boatwright, I hate to interrupt you but there is a gentleman here to see you."

"Did he give you his name?"

She whispers, "He's not sharing that with me, but he appears to be a bit anxious. I told him you were in study mode, but he is persistent. What shall I do?"

"I'll come out."

I put down my sketching pencil and take a deep sigh to allow my tension over this interruption to uncoil. I look at the postcard-size frame next to the monitor and re-read my antidote for such times:

> *"True ministry is all about the interruptions in life,* yours, as well as theirs."

Stepping into the hall, I am abruptly met by a very tan man dressed in bright orange golf shorts and a shamrock-green polo shirt, grinning widely.

"Reggie, what are you doing here?" I exclaim as all my sternness from being interrupted melts into pure joy at this pleasant surprise. "Come in! Come in!" I exclaim as I give this arrival a big bear hug. I look over his shoulder at Elizabeth, who winks and grins.

As we make our way into the counseling area and sit down on the sofa, Reggie begins to chatter.

"Max offered me something—tickets to the Masters—and I couldn't resist. His only requirement was for me to pick them up in person at his office—the tricky bait that brought me back to town. Couldn't resist the chance to drop in on you and say, 'Hi!'"

"Gosh, Reggie, it's been several years since I've heard from you. You sort of dropped off the radar! Bring me up to date. You look fabulous, I must say, all tanned and fit. Lost a few pounds, I see."

"And a bit of hair on top," Reggie confesses with a big smile. "But life is good. I'm living in Vero Beach now. Get to play golf almost year-round."

"Didn't know you were into golf, Reggie."

"Neither did I, until I took the time to try it. Found out I love it, perhaps more than it loves me at times."

"Vero Beach?"

"Yeah, can you believe it? When I'm not golfing, I'm fishing."

"So, life is good for you?"

"Good indeed."

"So, how did you end up in Florida?"

"You might say that is where I landed. I took off from here as soon as the doctor released me and found a rehab place for my leg wound in Savannah. Liked the weather and the coast and just started making my way south, trying to get some distance from Verona. I can tell you all the good fishing spots along the Intracoastal between here and the Jupiter Inlet in South Florida."

"I heard from the Verona grapevine that you sold the shop to Spike."

"Yeah, my half after Bonnie and I split up. Spike swung a good deal with the SBA for a loan, using his wife's name in the new ownership to get a special allocation for women-owned businesses. Turns out she was the leak to the newspaper where she worked. She couldn't pass up the temptation to give her boss, who happened to be the editor, an inside scoop on family business. So I walked away with a few grand, a fraction of what I had once been offered. Went through most of that over the next three years, but saved enough to pick up a franchise, or part of one, in Vero. It's one of those instant print and copy shops, with shipping and private mailbox deals. I plan to put in about fifteen hours a week just to monitor the operation and spend the rest of my days on the links or the water."

"And how is the rest of the family?"

"Bonnie moved quickly with the divorce proceedings. Neither of us was in the mood to fight. It soon became clear what had been going on in the background. The offer I had received from Gannett didn't just come about because Cornelius was such a great print shop. It turns out it was an introduction arranged and encouraged by Arnold, the paper salesman who had connections with the CEO of Gannett. Turns out that was not the only connection Arnold had. He had been *shagging* Bonnie for several years. The plan, as she confessed, was for the business to sell, she would take her half of the proceeds when she split, and the two of them would run off into the sunset together with their suitcases stashed full of cash, then live happily ever after. When the deal fell through, she had already committed herself to the divorce and to Arnold, who had already divorced his wife of twenty years, but left him totally broke. So they still ran off together, but with a whole lot less cash. She still owns half of Cornelius Printing as a silent partner and gets a share of whatever profit it produces.

"And I am sure you heard about Jerome."

"Yes, that came out in bits and pieces over time."

"Yeah. That was quite remarkable, what Spike did for that boy, taking him in. Even offered him a share of the business. But he's in the Marines now, doing quite well in military intelligence."

"That's nice to know. So, you're going to the Masters. What a thrill that must be."

"Indeed. I've been trying to get tickets ever since I started playing. Can't wait to walk those links and see the action in person."

A pause surfaces naturally, with both of us beginning to feel that the conversation is quickly nearing completion. The past has been updated. Only the details necessary for southern decorum have been revealed. I see the opportunity to close out and return to my sermon preparation.

"Well, Reggie, it is certainly good to see you. I am pleased it is all turning out okay for you."

"Indeed it has, Preacher, much of it because of your care for me during some tough times. I'll never forget what you did for me. But…" he pauses and looks down, "I have one more favor to ask of you."

"What do you need, Reggie?"

"Will you marry me? I mean, will you conduct a wedding for me, a marriage ceremony?" he stammers.

"Wow… tell me more," I reply, then quickly rise and go to the intercom. "Elizabeth, will you please bring us some coffee? If I remember right, Reggie takes his with sugar and two creams?" I turn to Reggie, who nods in affirmation.

CHAPTER THIRTY-NINE

Reggie takes the hot mug from my hand. "It's Molly. Molly Squires. Can you believe it?"

"No kidding! For real? I lost track of her. Last I heard, she was in South Alabama with her sister. How did you two meet up?"

"Preacher, you wouldn't believe it. We met on MatchesStruckin-Heaven.com. Turns out I was camping out at a friend's condo in Sebastian, that's near Vero Beach, and she was living in Vero. We struck up a friendship six months ago and before you know it, we were in love and started living together. We want to make it right, so we're tying the knot. We would both be honored if you would be so kind as to conduct the ceremony."

"Well, Reggie, I'm flattered. I am also very happy for you both. And I gladly accept the assignment with joy. Where will you have the ceremony? In your local church in Vero?"

"Well, Jon, that's another confession. We're not really involved in a local church. Neither one of us have been regular in attendance since we left Verona. Oh, we've visited around a bit. But to tell you the truth, we are exhausted with church. I say we, but actually it's me. I don't want to sit on another church committee for the remainder of my life. Don't get me wrong, Brother Jon. You were a good pastor to me, and you still are tops in my mind. But I realized much of what I was doing in the church had a lot to do with my family ties, to look good in my parents' eyes, to carry on the Cornelius tradition at The Hill. As I got older, I began to resent all the time I was spending at the church that I could be spending at the office or with my family. But then, I stayed involved because it seemed to be the business thing to do."

He takes another sip of coffee and then continues.

"Some of the reality that hit me when I had been gone from this town for a few months included admitting to myself that I did not really miss the church. I missed some of my friends and business acquaintances, not the church. Of course, I missed having an occasional good sermon from you that made me think, but I did not miss the politics, the bickering over finances or carpet colors or whether to replace the boiler this year or next. For the first time in my life— for the past several years—I have felt a freedom I had never experienced before."

"Tell me more, Reggie."

"Well, I remember some long conversations I had with you back when all of the business-selling agonies and Spike's demands were driving me insane. You said something about grace. You asked if I had ever experienced grace in my life. I could not recall a single instance at the time. But that question haunted me, at least the sorry answer I gave you. I have to say, looking back now, there were touches of grace I could not recognize. But I hadn't allowed them to make a difference in me. I'm rambling here, Preacher, so bear with me."

"I'm tracking with you, Reggie. Go on."

"It came to me recently, in Vero, when I ran into Molly and we started sharing our lives together, our journey. I was not completely forthcoming a minute ago when I said I had acquired a little franchise for office processing in Vero. The truth is I don't have a dime to my name. I have no debt, but little else. The franchise is in

Molly's name, and she is the one who put up the funds to pay the franchise fee. We are going to run the business together as soon as we get back from our honeymoon. All that to say I wouldn't have a pot to pee in if it wasn't for her generosity. She is a graceful woman. And I'm one lucky guy.

"So, will you still marry us, even if we are not all tied up in a local church?"

"It would be my pleasure, Reggie. Let me know the dates and location. We'll make it a grand celebration of life, a new beginning."

Reggie leaves with a promise to get back with the details of the wedding after conferring with Molly, and I return to my writing desk to continue the preparation for Sunday's sermon. I notice a different feeling about myself. Could it be a touch of envy?

CHAPTER FORTY

I t is the First Sunday of Pentecost, early June, which falls later than normal this year. As the sun threatens to break the eastern horizon over a flat Atlantic Ocean, Marsha rests her elbows on the tenth-floor balcony railing and takes in a deep breath of the salty humid air. As she pulls the collar of her bathrobe up around her neck and squeezes the fluffy lapels together across her chest, my arm settles on her right shoulder as I hand her a cup of coffee. We just stand there in silence, starting to squint a bit at the cresting orange ball. The gentle breeze ripples our hair.

Yesterday, we had a wonderful time with Reggie and Molly. The Reverend Dr. Jonathan Amos Boatwright had officially wed the couple in a private ceremony at a public sanctuary—the end of the dock extending into the Indian River at the yacht club where Reggie docked his restored 70-foot vintage tugboat, a wedding gift from Molly. The setting sun over the lagoon had painted pink cotton candy clouds in a deep blue sky. I was on my game, weaving together a very brief devotional about the wedding at Cana as a reminder that in life, sometimes God saves the best till last. Following the exchange of vows, the bride and groom had treated us to a fabulous meal of fresh orange roughy at the Cobalt beachside restaurant.

Now, the remainder of this holy day is for Marsha and me to enjoy without the kids. Any anxiety about their safety while at Pappa Joe and Nonnie's is interrupted by my tug on her robe, pulling her back into bed. After bathing together in the walk-through shower, we dress and make our way to the Lemon Tree for a breakfast with the other tourists who have scrapped their guilt about lack of worship attendance for a chilled mimosa. Over our order of fresh-baked croissants stuffed with eggs, cheese, and sausage and a side of cheese grits, we sit in silence gazing into each other's eyes, until Marsha expresses a thought. "We are going to have a great summer here, with the kids."

"Indeed," I reply through my stuffed cheeks. "Indeed."

I swallow then sip my coffee before continuing, "We'll need to set some routine to allow me to write and do research. Dan, over at Holy Cross, has put me in touch with a snowbird couple to use their garage apartment overlooking the Indian River for my studio."

"My, that's another pleasant surprise. They just keep coming."

"So true. Who would have thought Reggie and Molly would give us their place for the summer while they tour the Rhine on their honeymoon? And who would have thought the timing would match my sabbatical?"

"I suspect Reggie had some of that scheduling in mind. Did you think he had something to do with Conley asking you to be the adjunct professor for their MDiv/MBA program?"

"No, that came from Dr. Kostopoulos. Which reminds me, I need to order some books for delivery to our condo address."

"Okay. I'll remind you tomorrow! Let's have another round of mimosas and celebrate Sunday."

CHAPTER FORTY-ONE

On the first Sunday in August, which happens to be the Eleventh Sunday after Pentecost, and the first Sunday after concluding my sabbatical, I, The Reverend Dr. Jonathan A. Boatwright, tanned and in my right mind, stand in the midst of my congregation with the Gospel According to Luke, Chapter 12, beginning with verse 13 opened before me. I read aloud these words,

> *"Someone in the crowd said to him, 'Teacher, tell my brother to divide the family inheritance with me.'"*

I continue reading the selection to its conclusion, close the Gospel, and state the formula.

"The Gospel of our Lord Jesus Christ," to which the congregation responds, "Praise to you, Lord Christ."

As the parishioners are seated, I step down to the center aisle and deliver my sermon.

THE END

 obert Moon's wide ranging professional journey encompasses successful careers as a clergy person, a business executive, and a wealth manager. His passion is training clergy to relate to their parishioners where faith, business, wealth, and inheritances intersect.

Moon conducts workshops for clergy and seminary students to help them address their personal struggles with finance, business, and wealth while ministering to the disenfranchised and the poor. He has published two related books: *My Pastor, My Money, and Why We're Not Talking—Bridging the Gap Between Pastors and Those with Wealth* (2012), a non-fiction guide to facilitate conversations, and *In the Shade of the Sycamore Tree—Ministers Reflect the Subject of Wealth,* (2015), a collection of seventeen essays written by clergy persons representing several denominations.

In *All Saints Intersection—A Memoir* (2014), a private publication for his two sons, he explores his own journey beginning with a childhood surrounded by an inner city ministry to the homeless, the addicted, and the incarcerated. In sharp contrast to this childhood familiar with poverty, Moon has served as pastor and executive in some of the wealthiest enclaves of our nation. These contrasting venues of poverty and wealth underscore the challenge of today's ministry—balancing the diversity that embraces differences in race, ethnicity, and economic status.

Since 2006, he has been a partner in Heritage Financial, LLC, a wealth management firm in Gainesville, Virginia. His education includes a liberal arts degree in sociology from Georgia Southern University, Statesboro, GA; a Master of Divinity degree from Southwestern Baptist Theological Seminary, Fort Worth, TX; a Doctor of Ministry degree from Southern Baptist Theological Seminary,

Louisville, KY, and a MBA from the University of Colorado-Denver.

Robert is available for workshops, seminars, and one-on-one private consultations that seek thoughtful reflection on how faith, business, wealth and inheritance intersect in real life experiences. He and his wife reside in the pastoral countryside of Northern Virginia. More information is available at www.JRobertMoon.com

ACKNOWLEDGMENTS

To the individuals who supported this journey through multiple drafts: Dr. Daniel H. Kroger, Dr. Edward V. Jones, William Hornbuckle, Dr. Brent Strawn, and the writing artists of the Wednesday evening Write and Critique gathering at selected restaurants in Warrenton, Virginia.

To the early readers: Jan Cason, Lynn Ailor, Dallas Stallings, Jim Strickland, Rachel Lackey, Howard Roberts, Blake Gooch, Julie Covington, Tony Tedeschi, Matthew Brennan, Rebecca Burtram, and Tom Lippert, who allowed me to test my concept in the earliest versions and provided honest reactions and corrective guidance toward the final version.

To Dr. John Killinger, who was the first to give feedback and remained a constant source of support through frequent lunches.

To the study group—Lee Owsley, Terry Owsley, Marie Moore, Edward Jones, Marionette Jones, Philip Mulford, and Mark Cooke—for the Sunday evenings in our home testing the characters Jon, Reggie, and Spike and the sanity of their creator.

To the Blue Mountain Winery, the Barrel Oak Winery both of Delaplane, Virginia, The Porches of Norwood Virginia, The Sabbath House of Bryson City, North Carolina, and their respective staff for providing support and silence, cloistered space and venue, libations and scenery, from tabletops and desks in the varied writing retreats for this composition.

To the loblolly pines of the South harvested into pulp and paper on which were printed too many drafts or sample versions.

To Pat Ennis of Horatio Publishing Company, Nokesville, Virginia, Ruth Schwartz, editor and Kristin Kim, freelance editor, for their creative and technical skills that brought form and polish to what is now before your eyes.

To my partners and staff at Heritage Financial, LLC, for allowing me the time and space to pursue my calling and avocation and the freedom to test my creativity.

To the client, who shall remain anonymous, whose journey with sudden wealth ignited my passion for pastoral care in the context of wealth and began my journey toward this publication.

To my wife, best friend, and editor-in-chief, Mariann Lynch, for holding me accountable to my ramblings over long breakfasts on the porch, fireside chats in snowy weather, and late night discourses, yet provided unwavering support and encouragement throughout this multi-year project.